Lunch at the Igloo
and Other Stories

D0801931

Lunch at the Igloo and Other Stories

A Tribute to the Great Depression

Stories by Paul Huling

selected by Don Huling
with additional chapters
by Don Huling

Hither
Page
Press

Princeton,
Illinois

Editor: Paula Morrow
Book Designer: Ron McCutchan
Printed in the United States of America

Library of Congress Control Number: 2008939171

ISBN-13: 978-0-9798332-2-9

The stories on pages 22, 25, 34, 40, 42, 47, 63, 70, 75, 79, 96, 109, 126,
157, 160, 177, 179 originally appeared in Good Old Days magazine.

Dedicated to the memories of
the good times we had during the hard times,
when we were old enough to do our share
but young enough to believe the world
was full of undiscovered promise . . .
and there was no greener spot on earth
than the one where we lived.

CONTENTS

HIGH SCHOOL ADVENTURES

WAR YEARS AND BEYOND

APPENDIX: WHO'S WHO
AND WHAT WAS WHERE

PREFACE

TIME WAS GOOD to me when I was born in 1927. Dad had a good job as Plant Engineer for the Alpha Portland Cement Company in La Salle. He had purchased an almost new three-bedroom house at 744 Marquette Street a couple of years before I was born. He bought a brand-new 1929 Model A Ford—a four-door sedan with a luggage trunk—when I was two. We lived in a modest neighborhood where almost every house had kids about the same age as the four kids in my family.

When I was two and a half years old, a sellers panic caused the Great Depression. This would influence my life forever. In September 1929, before the October market crash, a study revealed that 60 percent of U.S. citizens had annual incomes of less than two thousand dollars, which was estimated as the bare minimum to supply the basic necessities of life. By 1932, wages were 60 percent less than in 1929. My dad was lucky. He was able to keep his job with a 50 percent cut in salary. That still placed us somewhat above the 1929 average minimum to supply the basic necessities.

Although I grew up during the Great Depression, I had everything a kid needed, and more. But I do remember things that can be looked back on as experiences of the Depression years.

PART I

A HAPPY CHILDHOOD

THE BASEMENT BREWERY

ON HOT SUMMER days back in the '30s, when my brother Don and I delivered newspapers together, we often took a short break at Baird's Grocery Store for a bottle of ice-cold root beer. One day as we drank our pop, brother Don noticed a tiny bottle on the grocer's shelf—the small size of it was what attracted his attention. It was a bottle of root beer extract.

"Just think," said Don as he read the fine print on the label, "for fifty cents we could make a whole case of root beer! What a bargain!" We couldn't pass it up, so we pooled our meager funds and bought the little bottle of brown substance.

That very summer evening, Don and I went into the brewing business in the basement of our house. We gathered up twenty-four bottles that Mom used for canning juice and found some bottle caps plus the press used to squash the caps on the bottles. We were on our way.

The directions were simple, as I remember them: Extract plus sterile bottles plus brewer's yeast plus bar sugar plus boiling water. Mix ingredients, fill bottles, cap, and wait seven days.

Due to circumstances, we modified the directions. The bottles looked clean enough, so we just rinsed them out. Mom had yeast to make bread, so we "borrowed" one square. Bar sugar? We mixed what table sugar and powdered sugar Mom had, leaving enough for

Don in 8th grade

breakfast, but we didn't really measure because we had no scale. Boiling water was out! It was too warm a night to heat up water in the old copper kettle.

We had a few problems. The yeast wouldn't dissolve in cold water. We lit a few matches under a tin cup of water and yeast, but that did no good. So we broke the cake of yeast into twenty-four pieces and placed one piece in each bottle. That worked so well we divided up the sugar into the bottles, added the extract mixed with water, capped the bottles, and gave each one a thorough shaking. The yeast turned to a gooey liquid and settled on the bottom, so we shook some more and figured that it would take a week to dissolve—thus the week's delay called for in the instructions.

About five days later at breakfast Dad asked us what our project was down in the basement. We'd hardly had time to respond when there came a noise from the basement that sounded like a popgun, then another. Our root beer!

"Basement Brewery" painting, 75th birthday present to Don from grandsons Dave and Doug Bratton.

The yeast must have been nearly dissolved. Not all of the bottles exploded. Don and I cleaned up the sticky, smelly mess, being careful not to get near the remaining bottles. It was a great joke around the house for the next couple of days. Mom tried to explain to us the differences between brewer's yeast and baking yeast, bar sugar and table sugar, plus sterilization of bottles and boiling water. Oh well, there were other opportunities ahead anyway.

The Plumbers

I NEVER NOTICED, but I imagine my mother had gray hair long before her time was due. She had three sons, about eighteen months' spacing in age. What one of them couldn't think of to do, two others could think of. Luckily, the three of us seldom put our heads together. My father called that a blessing.

Paul, September 1940

One day, when I was about twelve, I decided I weighed more than my oldest brother, Don. I stood on the new bathroom scale and loudly announced my newly acquired weight. It was less than 110 pounds, I'm sure, because I didn't weigh 120 until I was old enough to know better than what was about to transpire.

So Don got on the scale and loudly announced that he weighed more than me. I couldn't believe it; Don was the "runt of the litter." I must weigh more. It was a trick of some kind—it had to be! So I looked real close at the reading on the scale and noticed it wavered plus or minus a pound or two. Then I spotted one of his fingers hooked under the bathroom sink gently lifting up, thereby pushing him down on the scale.

Wise to his trickery, I got back on the scale again and tried the same stunt. Of course it didn't fool Don, but I made the scale register about 150 pounds.

Now this was where we put our heads together and came up with a most brilliant idea! If we both got on the scale and lifted up on the sink, we could max out the reading on the scale.

We'll never know if that is what we did or not, because the sink came off the wall! With the sink came the faucets, and without faucets the pipes in the wall had no reason at all to retain the pressurized water they were supposed to contain.

Of course we were in our undershorts at the time. The water was cold, very cold. It shot out in a spray that one could not escape—especially when one was trying to push the sink back into place like nothing had happened.

And brother Don took off running through the house, leaving me to try to squeeze the leaks, one hand on hot and one hand on cold. The floor was flooded with water. The towel chest was covered with sprayed water; the walls, toilet, bathtub, everything in the room was soaked, and my brother left me there by myself to account to Mother, who had become curious as to what was going on.

All she said as she opened the bathroom door to peek in was "Fix it!" and she shut the door.

Then, miraculously, the water quit spraying, and I heard Don yell, "Is it off?" He had run down to the basement and shut off the main water valve.

The rest of that day, Don and I had our work cut out for us. We learned how to hook up a sink to a wall: the hot and cold fixtures and the drain. We also cleaned the bathroom quite thoroughly. The bright spot of our day was that when we turned the water back on, there were no leaks!

Mom had a lot of towels to launder that day, and Dad inspected our work quite carefully but said nothing to his two boys who had put their heads together with a great idea that didn't pan out. He might have been just a tad proud of Don, who knew where to shut the valve off in an emergency. To this day I know where the main water shutoff is in that house.

First Kisses

I GREW UP in a small town during the Great Depression. The kids on the block where I lived played together. See map, page 192. There were twenty of us who grew from being the smallest kid, hanging around till a game or a team needed one more body and finally let us play, until we were grown up—or at least thought we were. We were never a gang, never malicious, didn't fight, and truly cared for one another as we grew up. We seldom had any money, either.

Our block was different from most I've ever seen. It had two alleys: one cut the block in half and was paved; the other cut one of the halves in half and was cinder. The paved alley was called Seventh Place, and four houses were built there in such a way that the front of the houses faced Seventh Place and the backs of the houses met the cinder alley. Two houses had no grass yard at all; the other two had very small yards.

There were no fences on our block. The area behind all the houses was more like a park where all the kids could play than lawns where children were restricted. Mothers and fathers could either see or hear what the kids were doing without leaving their houses.

We played baseball on Seventh Street where the curbing was not too high and the bricks were nice and level. We rode trikes, scooters, wagons, roller skates, and bicycles around the entire block on good sidewalks. Only on Seventh Street was the sidewalk paved, our first choice for roller-skating; all the rest were brick, like the streets.

When it was dark, we gathered under the streetlight on Seventh Place. That light was perfectly centered in the block and lit up the entire neighborhood. On moonless nights the light cast shadows in which we could hide as we played our hiding games. By the streetlight we played Tap, Tap the Ice Man and Kick the Can. Both games required someone to be It and count while everyone else ran and hid behind houses, bushes, posts, or just shadows. The It person had to leave the streetlight pole or the tin can, which was Home, and find someone, then return to the pole or can before the found person could run Home Free. If It traveled too far from Home, those hiding could also run Home Free. But in Kick the Can, if some had already been caught and one still hiding got to the can and kicked it, everyone who had been caught was set free while It ran after the can and returned it to its spot under the streetlight. I learned to hide quite well playing these games.

One day the girls announced they had heard of a new game called Spin the Bottle. We sat in a circle as one of the girls whirled the bottle centered amongst us. It stopped pointing at a girl, so that was a void spin. It next stopped pointing to one of the boys, so she kissed him.

"Aagh! She kissed him!!" we boys yelled.

Then it was the kissed boy's turn to spin the bottle. So

now the game became more interesting. Maybe this game had possibilities. That was the day the kids in my neighborhood learned we were very poor kissers—but we had a wonderful time practicing our skills. We would announce a Clark Gable kiss, a Gregory Peck, Lana Turner, or Hedy Lamarr, before the extravagant act took place. There was even the Roy Rogers horse Trigger kiss! Roars of laughter would burst forth and, after the kiss, the kissee would tell the kisser whether the kiss was worthy—with exaggeration!

Of course, this all took place in the front yard of one of the girls, and her mother was supervising, unbeknownst to us—or thought she was, till her hysterical laughter gave her away.

We soon outgrew the game. I doubt if any of us remember who we kissed first, but I do know we still kid each other about those lousy kisses.

Jackknives

WHEN I WAS a boy, a jackknife was a handy tool. Jackknives came in handy sizes from very small with 1" blades to large with 4" blades. But most jackknives had two blades side by side—a small one about 1 1/2" long and a long blade about 2 1/2" long. Some of my friends had a jackknife for each pair of high-cuts they bought. (High-cuts were calf-high leather shoes.) There was a little leather packet sewn on the high-cuts where the knife was stored.

The jackknife I owned had a green handle. My dad showed me how to keep it sharp enough to shave the hair off my arm. Learning that meant I wanted to keep it sharp, and in order to keep it sharp I didn't use it to cut just any old thing; it had to be something important or I wouldn't use my good knife. Being sharp also meant I had respect for its sharpness. My dad was pretty smart that way. I kept my knife to myself, in my pocket.

But then I had a dull knife also. The dull knife was used for playing a game with boys from the neighborhood. I think we called it mumbly-peg. There may have been another game called that, but as I remember, we made up our own rules. The winner of the game used the jackknife to drive a wooden matchstick into the ground. He got three taps. He used the knife handle as the hammer head and the short blade as the handle. The loser had to remove the matchstick from the dirt using only his teeth. This must have been where the name mumbly-peg came from. But, as I said, we made up our own games and rules in those days, so we called our game baseball, although we played it with a jackknife.

First the short blade was fully opened; then the long blade was half opened, positioning it at 90 degrees to the handle and the short blade. The knife was then positioned with the blade and handle resting on the ground. Then the knife was flipped into the air so it made a couple of revolutions before it landed. If it landed on the large blade and handle, it was called a single base hit. We all kept track of runners. If it landed on the long blade, it was a double. If it landed on the short and long blades, it was a triple. If it landed on the small blade, it was a home run! If it fell over, that was an out.

We spent hours playing baseball. The first person to get a score of ten runs across home plate won the game, and the loser was the person with the fewest runs.

Alas, my grandchildren will probably never learn to play baseball with a jackknife. They can't even carry one to school. How can they sharpen a pencil?

Toys My Dad Made for Us
by Don Huling

IN THE MIDDLE of the Great Depression, money was hard to come by—especially money for such nonessentials as toys. So my dad decided to make his own toys for his three competitive boys.

The first toy he made when I was still quite small was an erector set. He made it from wood trim 3/4" wide by 1/4" thick by 3' long with 3/16" holes drilled every inch apart. We built a wooden windmill, but this toy was too passive for three active boys. We needed something with which we could challenge each other.

The next toy was a multigame board. The board was about 3' square. On one side was a checkerboard, and on the other side was a game we played with red and green wooden "shooters." These were about an inch in diameter and 1/2" tall with the core drilled out. In the center of this side of the game board was a well

"Look what Santa Brought Us!" Alice and Don

about 2" in diameter and 3/8" deep. The object was to score points by flipping the shooter into this indentation, using only your middle finger. Of course, when one player succeeded in doing this, his opponent went all out to knock the first player's piece off the board—often with a vengeance. To complicate things a little more, twelve pins in the shape of a 9" square surrounded the well. The pins had rubber bumpers on them, which added to the challenge of knocking out your opponent. We played this game many a winter day when we couldn't get outside.

Sails and kites. Down near the Alpha Cement Company was a lake called Goose Pond. It wasn't really a lake; it was a spring-fed backwater of the Illinois River. Some sportsmen had built a hunting lodge on the west end of the lake and would shoot ducks when the hunting season opened. The pond would freeze solid later on, and that's when my dad would pile a bunch of us kids in the Model A Ford and drive down to enjoy the winter sports. Bill Gebhardt would often be included.

We all had ice skates, so one sport we all enjoyed was ice hockey. When the water froze overnight without any snow falling, it was slick as glass. We had some good races around the pylons, and invariably some kid would fall down racing around the curve and go sliding on his back.

But the best event was ice sailing. Dad came up with this idea to build a large 4' by 8' sail from two 1" by 2" by 10' pieces of lumber joined together in the middle with a 1/4" bolt. We made a big X, then strung good strong twine around the outside to make a 4' by 8' frame. Around the twine we folded and glued heavy brown wrapping paper Dad brought home from the plant. That was our sail.

The one and only time we tried out this new toy of Dad's, the ice was just right. The wind was blowing from the west to the east, strong and steady. Dad had some of the other kids, who were making a big fuss, try it out first. They just didn't seem to get the hang of it. Dad explained to me the art of leaning into the wind with the sail and tacking back and forth across the pond. After a few times, I was off sailing across the lake.

Remember how I mentioned the lake was spring-fed? The springs were down at the east end, so I didn't worry about the open water as I crisscrossed the lake. But my dad did! He started shouting for me to be careful because I was getting too close to the open water. I finally realized I was in trouble, but how to stop this thing?! I finally threw it up into the air, and off it went—right into the water! Dad never built another ice sail. Too dangerous, he said.

Dad loved to build kites and taught John and Paul and me how to do it. His dad and Uncle Charlie had shown him how to do it when he was a kid back on the farm. Our most reliable kite was a three-sticker. Two 3' and one 2' stick were joined together near the middle then separated to form a six-sided figure. We strung string around the outside edges, then cut and pasted brown paper around the string to make the kite. We had to add a tail to this design to make it fly. The tail was simply a long piece of string with folded newspaper tied in place every foot or so.

The most fun kite was Dad's airplane design. It had a 1' by 4' wing with a 6" by 12" tail. It would fly almost straight up overhead, then spill the wind and head straight down. The only way to get control of it was to run as fast as you could into the wind and hope a tug on the string would straighten it out. One day the kite got away from us because the string broke from a sudden blast of wind. That day we went running for it.

Dad continued to build toys even after all of us kids left home and he had retired to the farm. One game he invented was open-field croquet, and his most elaborate toy was the high-lo teetertotter.

Judy Abraham from Argentina was living with us when we first played Dad's version of croquet. He used large 8" rubber balls, heavy wooden mallets, and 3' long iron straps that could be bent into wickets. The game could be set up and played on any terrain, and the court could be as long or short as desired. We took one of these sets back to La Salle and played it one weekend out at Deer Park.

The high-lo was a unique teetertotter. The kids on either end always remained parallel to the ground. Dad accomplished this by using a parallelogram design. One summer when all of us were out at the farm, he introduced it to us. He was anxious to find out what we thought of it. David and Douglas found it hard to get on and off. I found too many pinch points to make it safe. As far as I know, Dad retired this toy shortly after we left for home.

Maxwell

MAXWELL WAS A collector. He collected all kinds of "stuff" and "things." Max was the first kid on the block to have collections. I didn't even know people collected things till I knew Max. I think Max learned from Abby, his mother, about collecting.

The Freudenburgs moved next-door to us on Marquette Street about 1935. Mr. Freudenburg was a photographer and had a studio above one of the stores on First Street in La

Salle. He did the photography, and his wife tinted the pictures people wanted in color. (I still own some of the pictures taken at the Freudenburg studio when I was about four years old.) When the Depression forced Mr. Freudenburg (Maximilian) to give up renting downtown, he moved his studio to the basement of his house on Marquette Street. It never thrived there, but not much thrived during the Depression.

What did thrive in the Freudenburgs' basement were the neighborhood boys. Mr. F. gave Max a roll of moving picture film that was well beyond its shelf life. Max knew enough about film that he could cut the movie film into lengths and roll them onto a used spool, and we all had free film. Max also knew how to develop and print, so we were in business!

Because the movie film was narrow, we had to take narrow pictures when lining up our viewfinders. Mr. F. gave us lessons on the importance of backgrounds and focusing properly. Of course, the cameras we kids owned never cost us more than fifty cents, so, for us, focus meant don't get too close. After we had used up Mr. F.'s solutions

Maxwell Freudenberg

and print paper, he was officially out of the photo business, but we kids were well versed in photography.

Maxwell's first collection that I recall was stamps. He and my brother Don traded cancelled stamps they purchased by the bag at the dime store. Sometimes the stamps were from foreign countries!

Indian head pennies, and coins in general, were another thing Max collected. There was one customer on my brother Don's paper route who paid us (I helped) fifteen cents a week, for weeks, with Indian head pennies. We dutifully saved them for Max, and if he didn't have fifteen cents that week, he would pay us later. Max had many coin cards full of coins, except for a space or two of the hard ones to find. I'll bet a nickel he had them all his life.

Little wooden puzzles were another item Max collected. He had cubes, spheres, and other shapes of wooden puzzles, which he would loan me until I had mastered them. He liked discussing each piece as we studied them. He also had a bent nail puzzle collection, but his thoughts and mind were way beyond the challenges they offered.

Maxwell sold *Radio Guide,* a weekly publication that had previews of radio programs. He generally stood on First Street, in front of his father's photo studio, or at the corner of First and Marquette Streets, to sell his wares. He didn't have a paper route that was a rain-or-shine business; he could stand in the doorway of a downtown business and sell his wares. A *Radio Guide* cost a lot—a nickel, or a dime—and Max made good profit selling them. He kept quiet about his *Radio Guide* business because he sort of had a monopoly in our town and didn't want competition. He also chose the best corner in town to hawk his wares.

When Max bought a bicycle, it was a Montgomery Ward with a light in front, a horn in the tank, a carrier on the back, and a basket for his *Radio Guide* sack. It was black-and-white, with chrome rims and whitewall tires. He had saved a long time for that bike, and every now and then he would shine it up till it looked like new. He didn't take care of it daily, just now and then. If I had to guess, I'd say Max took care of his cars the same way when he was older.

There was one summer evening I remember very well, when Maxwell educated a group of us boys from the neighborhood about sex. Max had studied the subject thoroughly

Don leads Paul, Max, and Fred (Schmoeger) in the Boy Scout Oath.

and spoke without notes. He followed the cycle of sex from a sperm through the birth of a child. It wasn't a "how to have sex" lesson he taught us, it was the miracle of conception and life. We were sitting on the front porch steps of Allen Schermerhorn's home when Max recited this bit of knowledge, and Allen's mother was in the living room where she could hear. When Max was finished, she came out on the porch and told Max that he had given the best presentation she had ever heard. I still remember it.

Max was four days older than my brother John. They went to the same schools for twelve years, the same church, and played the same games with the same kids from the neighborhood. One Sunday I ended up in their Sunday school class with Max and John's teacher talking to her class about praying. It was an all-boys class with a woman—I believe Mrs. Wilson—as teacher. At the end of the class session she asked who amongst them would offer a prayer. Max did. I have long forgotten the prayer, but will not forget its sincerity.

Where there was mischief or trouble, Max would not be there, as he was just not a problem for anyone. I have pictures taken about 1942 with Max and me in our Boy Scout

uniforms collecting books for the soldiers at war or alumi-
num pots and pans for a scrap drive, and on an outing at
Bailey's Falls, a place where we used to hike (which was later
mined over to obtain the limestone).

Max went to war in 1944; I went in 1945. We didn't see
each other again until 2001. There are gaps of time in Max's
life I don't know much about, but I do know he was a great
friend to have for a lifetime.

There is one more thing to mention about Max. He was
never one to file things away carefully; in fact, to many of us,
he was sort of messy. The gathering of things that took his
interest was voluminous! Maybe he knew where everything
was, but I could never spot a pattern of orderliness. But that
was Max. The last time I saw him he was using a rented truck
to haul the many items he needed to make his vacation trip.
His motel room was so full of things, I wondered where he
would sleep! Yes, that was Max. And I never met a person so
well suited for his profession—Max was a patent attorney.

My Hobbies

MY FIRST MEMORY of spending an overnight at my
friend Tom's farm is when we woke up early one morning
and went to an enclosed porch where we could make noise
without waking up his mom or dad. Tom, an only child,
had a huge chest full of toys, more toys than all the toys my
brothers and I owned. But there was a problem with most of
Tom's toys—they were broken one place or another.

There was a metal fire truck that was really nice, except
one wheel was broken loose and the ladder was bent so that it
didn't work. I fell in love with it as I spent the morning trying
to fix it while Tom played with the toys that were not broken.

By the time Tom and I said good-bye that afternoon, he had given me a basketful of toys that needed fixing, and they were mine to keep! I tried and tried to fix them all, but my dad had to help me by showing me which tools to use and where to find them in the basement. One hobby was started that day.

Whenever Dad had a project to work on in the basement, I was there watching and learning. When I visited the farm, my grandmother and the hired man had many repairs to make on harnesses, wagons, plows, and other farm equipment. I was there.

My older brother made model airplanes from kits. I watched him make planes but didn't have an interest in kits; I made my own planes for free, from old slats I found in our basement.

One of our favorite toys was a mold for making lead soldiers. For a dime we could buy a pound of lead at Romanowski's junkyard at the corner of First and Bucklin Streets. We would heat the lead to the melting point on the stove Mom used to heat water. We had a neat array of soldiers. Then one day the surface under the mold was wet when Don poured hot lead into the mold, and the water exploded into steam, throwing molten lead on Don's hand. We never used the mold again, although Don recovered OK.

One very hot day, my sister, Alice, was practicing the piano and complained about how hot it was. I immediately went to work in the basement with my father's drawknife to produce a propeller just like the ones I had seen my brother make for airplanes, only the propeller I made was about 2' long and made from a shaved-down 2" by 2" piece of pine. I attached the propeller to an old washing machine electric motor. When I plugged it in, the propeller took off spinning and the heavy motor slid on the bench. I stopped the motor and then attached it to a flat board so I could clamp it to a chair, where it couldn't take off if I held the chair.

When I turned it on and pointed it at Alice, she had two problems. All her music blew away, and her hair wrapped around her head till she couldn't see. The entire room was a mess of blown sheet music and papers.

Later, when my dad saw what I had made, he took it apart and had a talk with me about safety. I had not realized that an out-of-balance propeller was a dangerous thing or that 2,000 rpm was too fast for a fan. Other than endangering my sister's and my lives, I had done a wonderful job of crafting a fine propeller, my dad said.

One day I bought a bicycle. We didn't have a bike at my house, mostly because there were four kids in the family. Four bikes would have been expensive, filled the garage, let us wander too far from home, plus maybe some more reasons. Not having bicycles kept my family together longer.

The bike I bought cost a dime. It was supposed to be all there, but I couldn't tell because all the pieces were in a wooden crate—that is, all the pieces except a pedal and two tires. That was OK. I didn't need tires and couldn't afford them even if I did get the thing put together.

Dad showed me how to adjust a bearing and what pieces to grease, but that's all. He didn't want it fixed and didn't really expect I would get it together. But I surprised him.

It was hard, and I mean hard—bumpy—to ride on brick streets without tires. Tires were worth maybe a dollar and the bike wasn't, so I rode on the rims. The bike seemed to slip out from under me when I tried to turn. There was also that missing pedal. And there were no brakes. . . . The way I stopped was to jump off the bike and let it crash.

About this time a friend of mine saw the bike and said he needed the chain. So I sold him the entire bike for fifteen cents. That was a great relief to my parents . . . and I had earned a profit.

Next I made a pushcart. One person sat on it and another person pushed. The only wheels I had were roller skates, so I disassembled a pair of roller skates to use the front half of the skates as front wheels and the heel part of the skates as rear wheels attached to a 2" by 4" rear axle.

To steer the pushcart, I used a two-by-four as a front axle long enough that one steered with the feet, with the assistance of a rope attached out near the wheels.

Stability was what I learned about with this project. The fool thing seemed to fall apart, especially if the one riding and being pushed ran into immovable objects, which seemed to happen every time we got it going good. This project ended when the buddy I was pushing ran the uncontrollable cart into the porch and ended up with a large sliver under his thumbnail. I told my friend to leave the splinter under his nail and in time it would fester and fall out. The gods were with me, because it worked and he didn't die of tetanus.

By now the basement was my favorite room, and my dad made sure there were nails, boards, and a junk box from which to search for materials. I won a birdhouse-building contest because I had made a birdhouse from a hollowed-out willow log. The house was very plain, but I attached a flashlight to it so the judges could see the wren's nest inside. I still make these birdhouses, and they still attract wrens.

I've never stopped making or fixing. One restaurant where my wife and I performed our music three days a month for years used to make up what they called a laundry list, which meant things for Laundry Fat (me) to fix when I came.

Paul's Barn

In fact, I've expanded. I now occupy the entire basement, a small room off the kitchen, and a three-story barn where I am removing the third-floor flooring to use the lumber to make furniture. I don't know for whom.

Tom's School—District 176, Nellis School

I'LL NEVER KNOW if it was Tom's mother or my mother who conceived the idea that when the public schools in La Salle had days off, that would be a good time for me to visit the Robinson farm north of town. Tom was—and still is—my good friend. If I visited him on a day that he had school, Tom went off to school with me in tow.

At first I thought that was going to be the pits, visiting a one-room country school where one teacher taught all grades. I'll spend the whole day with nothing to do but wait, I thought.

How wrong I was! After the first time or two at Tom's school, I actually looked forward to going!

I liked to go because I learned so much. The upper-grade students were not condescending; on the contrary, they were helpful to the lower grades, and the little kids looked up to them with great admiration. All eight grades helped each other. The school was a unit where each student cared for the others. I had never been in a school like that.

Getting to school was another experience. Instead of walking brick sidewalks as I did in town, Tom and I walked through the woods and fields along the creek. Some days, when the creek was too swift to cross, we walked the gravel road for about a mile.

One time, on our walk through the woods, we came upon an opossum that was "playing possum." When we described it to Tom's father, he told us what it was. We returned to the spot where we had seen it, and sure enough, it was gone.

In winter, we would arrive at the school to find that the teacher had already fired up the wood-burning stove to warm the room.

Tom's teacher never minded my visits. I wished she had been my teacher a time or two.

All students stood facing the flag for the Pledge of Allegiance. Then each class would take its turn to go to the front of the room where the students sat on the bench for their lessons. Everyone in the room could hear—and learn.

No wonder Tom's so smart, I thought. He'll hear this lesson eight times over before he graduates. And I only got to hear the lesson once; was that fair?

One day, lo and behold, the whole school had a geography lesson at once. First graders at Tom's school could find Cuba on a world map. Eighth graders could find cities like

Belem (in northern Brazil). No wonder Tom had fun with me, talking geography. I was a dummy compared to kids at his school.

BACK: **Wayne Black, Wesley Freebairn, Tom Freebairn, Loraine Crane, Miss Martha Rogowski, Loretta Crane, Wesley Black, Leo Dugosh;**
FRONT: **Tom Robinson (standing), Doris Crane, Donald Freebairn, Anna Jean Freebairn, Loraine Johnson, Ruth Hill, Dick Dudek, Eugene Dugosh.**

Tom's School

All in all, I'd say Tom received the superior education when we were growing up. It wasn't that I attended an inferior school; it was just that I was a boy who would have done better at his school than I did at mine.

The Curb Sitter

I ENJOYED SITTING on the curbing in front of our house at 744 Marquette Street and watching the many interesting people pass by. Marquette Street was made of bricks laid on edge. These made tires sing; one could tell if a car was approaching fast or slowly by the pitch of the noise the tires made on the bricks.

The sidewalk, which was behind me as I sat on the curb, was brick laid flat, smooth enough to rollerskate on; but if one hummed, one's voice sounded vibrato. Two elm trees on the parkway provided refreshing shade on warm summer days.

I tried to be sitting on the curb before the grocery truck arrived. "Red" Baird drove the old panel truck around the neighborhood, delivering orders that had been phoned in earlier that day.

Sometimes he was in a hurry as some housewife was waiting for his delivery to begin preparing what we would now call "slow food," because it sure wasn't fast food in those days. But if he wasn't in a rush, he would ask my mom if I could ride along for a little while as he made his deliveries.

I really loved to do that. I sat on an upside-down wooden box next to the driver's seat, which was the only seat in the truck. Red talked to me as we rode.

If I was with Red, that was great, but if he was rushed, I'd wait for Mr. Tieman. Mr. Tieman had a produce farm in nearby Spring Valley where he grew wonderful fruit and vegetables. Mother bought many vegetables from Mr. Tieman. Sometimes he had specials, and then Mom would buy large quantities for canning. I wasn't much interested in the veggies, but sometimes he would ask me to sample an apple from his truck.

Mr. Tieman's truck was beautiful! He must have washed it daily. Bright green with red wooden-spoked wheels, it was very, very old—so old, in fact, that it had well-oiled chains to drive the rear dual wheels. The truck had a bell like a streetcar's. There was a tall button on the floorboard of the truck, and when he depressed it, the bell clanged. Sometimes while he was stopped in front of our house, he would ask me to push the button "just one time" to alert the slower-moving housewives in the neighborhood.

If it was a nice day, not too hot, Mr. Neustadt would pass the house at 10 A.M. I didn't have a watch, but I learned that it was always 10 A.M. when Mr. Neustadt passed by. He rode his beautiful roan horse and he was dressed for show: a riding cap, riding britches, shiny black riding boots, and a black riding jacket with a white scarf puffing from the collar under his chin. He never looked at me—or anyone else—as he rode his fancy-stepping horse for his morning outing. But evidently he knew who I was, because when I was twelve, he hired me to run errands and make change for him while he talked to customers in his clothing store.

Then there was Mrs. Campbell. She had an electric car! She looked like she was sitting in the backseat as she silently glided down the street. The car was very tall; I think she could stand up inside. It had glass all around and curved glass at the four corners. Mrs. Campbell drove it so slowly that it made hardly any noise on the bricks.

One day Mrs. Campbell pulled up to the curb, and I had

to move. She was coming to our house! While she talked to Mother, I admired her car. Inside, beside the door, were flower vases with real flowers. The person in the "front" seat, if there were passengers, sat facing the driver, who faced forward. I think the car would go either direction depending on where the driver sat. There was no steering wheel—just a tiller like I had to steer my wagon. Mrs. Campbell was always dressed up, with a veil on her hat.

When I heard steel wheels coming down the brick street, I ran to the porch to watch. It was usually "gypsies." Horses pulled their tall-sided wagons. The wagons had windows with shutters, and the women and kids would look out the windows. The women wore loud clothing, with red bandannas over their hair. The kids looked like they could have used a bath, but they looked happy, like they didn't envy the rest of the world at all. These people were headed north of town, where there was a farm that welcomed them to camp. Today they would probably be called migrant workers.

Fire! When the sirens sounded, all of La Salle and even Peru, the adjoining town, could hear the Eighth Street Fire Department siren, which was only four blocks from my house. If I wasn't at the curbing, I would be at the corner of Eighth and Marquette (the house next-door), waiting and watching to see if the hook-and-ladder fire truck would pass.

That fire truck was so long that it required a steering wheel up front and a steering wheel in back to make it around corners! The ladders were long enough to reach the upper floors of the Kaskaskia Hotel, our town's tallest building.

Seeing the hook and ladder was one thing, but hearing it was quite another. It roared and spewed out huge amounts of blue smoke. Sometimes it backfired and coughed because it wasn't warmed up yet. I don't believe it had a muffler,

LaSalle's 1928 American LaFrance

because red-and-orange flames shot out as it roared down the streets.

On hot days I couldn't wait for the Callahan brothers to deliver ice. Each customer had a square card to place in a window. If the number 25 was on top, that meant 25 pounds of ice; if 100 was up, that was 100 pounds.

Our icebox held 50 pounds. The Callahans used an ice pick to pick around the circumference of a huge block of ice to crack off our 50-pound block. Then they carried it to the kitchen and deposited it in the icebox.

But while they were away from the truck, the neighborhood boys were scooping up the chipped ice on the bed of the ice truck to eat. The Callahans never minded unless some kid tried to chip a corner off a large block instead of picking up the scraps. Those brothers were strong, so I don't believe they had any trouble with kids, once they let the rules of the game be known.

At least once each summer, the sound of a small hand-bell announced the arrival of the little man who carried his workshop on his back. It didn't weigh much and it was foot-powered. As he stood on one foot, his other foot pumped a contraption that spun a stone that sharpened knives, scissors, and blades of any sort.

It seemed like his little bell could cut through any other noise, because all the women from both sides of the street left their homes with armloads of things, from paring knives to scythes, for the little man to sharpen. Of course, the ladies gathered and chatted as they waited.

The little man had a mustache, a conductor's hat, and a big smile. I doubt that he spoke English; his only communication was a smile.

About four times a day, a girl who had a crush on the boy next-door rode her bike as fast as she could down Marquette Street. That bike had a siren! Her idea was to make the siren scream, thereby attracting the attentions of her intended. I don't know if that panned out, but she stopped one day so that I could examine the siren. It was mounted on the bike so that when she pulled a string, the little wheel that ran the siren made contact with the front tire of the bicycle, causing the siren to spin. Sadly, either the romance ended, she got tired of racing down the street, or the siren wore out.

If someone, anyone, sat with me on the curb, we would play "red wire wheels." It seems Ford had come out with bright red spoke wheels, and it became a fad to update older Fords by painting their spoke wheels red. There was no hitting one another, or kissing, or any other action, except vying to be the first to shout out when we spotted any red wire wheels.

One winter day I was sitting on the curb, watching cars spin their wheels. The temperature was well below freezing, and it had rained. The rain froze when it hit the ground, and the bricks became thick with ice. It happened so fast that some people didn't realize the street was icy.

Mrs. Andrews was one of those unlucky souls. Her husband sold Goodyear tires, and their car was a brand-new Airflow Chrysler, a very large automobile. As she glided around the corner at Eighth and Marquette, her car slid in such a way that both of the wheels on the right side of the car hit the curb at the same time. The wheels couldn't take the side load, and they just folded over the curb till they looked like two wheels lying on the lawn.

When she got out of her car, she discovered that she couldn't walk without holding on to it. But by now the car was also icing up, so she just stood there and cried.

Later, much later, her husband retrieved the Chrysler. I don't remember how she got home; she only lived at Sixth and Marquette. She could have ice-skated home, because for two full days, motor traffic stopped and every kid with skates traveled the town freely, using the streets as a rink.

Ed Hack delivered our coal, and I watched him from outside, on the driveway. He pushed a metal chute into the basement window and, using a coal shovel, removed the coal from his truck. No matter how cold it was, Ed could work up a sweat. He'd be covered with black coal dust, as was the entire inside of our house when he was done.

This story wouldn't be complete if I didn't mention the walkers who passed my house. Many people walked because they owned no transportation. But one family walked for exercise every day.

Mr. and Mrs. Hahne ran the Hotel Kaskaskia on Second and Marquette Streets. They lived in the hotel and needed to get out once in a while with their two kids.

When I started curb sitting and watching, the Hahnes

Jean and Bill Hahne

only had one child—a little girl. They quite often walked all the way to Fourteenth Street. I know how far they walked because one day, I told my wife that when I was a kid, I would go all the way to Fourteenth Street just to pick up a stick so that I could run back with it as I held it against the tall iron fence at the corner of Roosevelt and St. Vincent's Avenue, just to hear the noise it made. She told me that she had done the same thing when she was on her walks with her mom and dad—my future in-laws, Mr. and Mrs. Hahne.

The Iron Fence, Roosevelt and St. Vincent's

Why do I remember all these people I watched while curb sitting? They are the people who helped form my character and my work ethic. As I sat on the curb and watched these people pass by, I could study each one's character, enabling me to pattern my own life as I grew older.

I believe I watched a wonderful parade.

What's in a Nickname?

WHEN AND WHERE I grew up, we used nicknames. Generally the nickname fit the character or personality of the individual pretty well. Some require a little explanation before they are understood. Here are a few nicknames of people I grew up with:

Gabby Gebhardt

Gabby. I had two friends called Gabby, because they were.

Flea. Not only small, but a fantastic sport. When Flea was about eight years old, the losing baseball team selected him from the little kids observing the game as pinch hitter, figuring a sure walk because the strike zone was so small. Flea drove in two runs and won the game.

Shady got into some shady deals and was so tall he cast a long shadow.

Liberty Bell was called that because he was half-cracked.

Dutch was close.

Blimp needed to lose his baby fat and did, but the name remained.

Soupy drove a car during and after the war that ran on faith but was really not fit for the junk pile.

Horatio got his name when the teacher called on him and he had actually read the assignment, "Horatio at the Bridge."

The teacher was in shock, and we students celebrated the event by pinning a new name on him. It stuck.

Beastie had no problem with violence, but the name somehow fit the smallest kid in our class.

Whoopde was a good-time fellow, always.

Slurpo was named by my brother, who taught her how to kiss. Just that simple, no more to the story.

Marblehead was a girl. The name fit.

Buttons was missing a few.

Hot Gob didn't like what some Scouts fed him so he spat it out . . . on them; I guess it was hot!

Uncle Bulgy was dean of men at our local college.

Foxy was football coach at the college.

Butch was coach of the high-school football team.

Bugsy was our biology teacher. She wore Coke-bottle glasses.

Jigs played end on the football team so well he went to college on a scholarship. When he ran, it looked like he was falling apart.

Bird Dog had a dog that attacked me. The police shot him . . . the dog, not Bird Dog. But Bird Dog claimed his dog was a bird dog, not an attack dog. We remained friends.

Rathead was my Sunday school teacher who never deserved to be called that, but we did anyway.

Shadow was too small to cast one.

The Count wore a suit one day and was forever after The Count. Every time he wore that suit his friends would run ahead of him and proudly proclaim, "Here comes The Count! Stand back!"

Pot didn't have one, and we didn't know pot would ever mean what it does today; it had something to do with a restroom experience.

Bates. We called him Master Bates. He liked to play with himself.

Joe the Butt Picker. Now he was smart, they told me; if you offered him a dime and a penny he would only take the penny because that way he had more than ten times the offers. Joe (we don't know if that was his real name) sat in front of the local movie theater where he would obtain his smokes for the day from men who threw theirs away! Offer him a new one or a pack and he'd turn you down. I never tried that, but I believe it.

And finally, my own nickname, Fat. It was given to me when I was a little kid with fat chubby arms. The name stuck, even after I slimmed down. My wife, Jean, uses it as a term of endearment.

It seems that behind every nickname is a story, and most nicknames fit the person.

The Boys' Room

OUR HOUSE HAD an unheated room above the garage. This room had windows on all four sides—a total of ten—that made it nice for hot summer nights. In the summer it was like sleeping outside. In the winter it was like sleeping outside. During the winter months, the door connecting the room to the house was kept closed unless the hand-fired coal furnace got too hot.

Dad would fire up the furnace every morning, and he'd bank the fire every night. Hot water was heated on the kitchen stove on washdays. Mother had a two-burner gas heater to heat the copper boiler. It felt great to have hot water vapors in the house on winter laundry days, but terrible in the summer.

The Boys' Room

Huling home at 744 Marquette Street. House #24 on map, page 192.

The first winter I spent in the room above the garage was in 1938. Don and I had talked Mom into letting us try it. I was eleven years old and Don was fourteen. Our brother John, who was between us in age, was recovering from rheumatic fever at my grandparents' farm in Ohio. It was up to Don and me to prove that the room would be healthy for all of us, including John.

Mom made up the bed with cotton blanket sheets, woolen covers, and about three quilts. For pajamas, she dyed oversized long flannel underwear bright red. Then she added heavy woolen knee-socks and knitted stocking caps. We were ready. Almost.

The final touch was at the kitchen range, where Don and I would heat a kettle of water to boiling, then pour it into a hot-water bottle. We would wrap it in a towel and then run and jump under the covers with it between us.

It didn't take long before our body heat, aided by the hot-water bottle, warmed the bed to sleeping temperature. Dad said we slept like bugs in a rug.

We dressed and undressed in the warm bathroom in the main house. Each night we would run into our room just long enough to get our clothes for the morning, and each morning we would return to the cold room after dressing just long enough to quickly make up the bed and retrieve the hot-water bottle.

One very cold morning, as we were making the bed, we couldn't find the hot-water bottle. We both searched under the covers of the double bed, but we couldn't locate it.

Then Don spotted it. It had fallen out of bed. I spotted it, too, on my side of the bed. In fact, we both spotted it—because when it fell out of bed, it had broken in half! One half was under Don's side, and one half was under mine. But there was no puddle on the floor because the hot-water bottle had frozen solid between us as we slept.

We didn't tell Mom.

When spring came, Mom and Dad had the room painted and papered, and they bought us a pair of double bunk beds so that each of us would have a bed of his own. Now we could even sleep a guest in our room. By now, John was healthy again, and he loved our new quarters.

When Mom said that she needed to buy two more hot-water bottles for us, we told her that we didn't need them. But we never told her what had happened to the first one.

Years later, I was in the U.S. Navy off the coast of New London, Connecticut, in the middle of winter. PC-522, my ship, had taken on fuel contaminated with water, so we were dead in the water—no main engines, no electricity, no water—and the temperature was near zero. Salt water was freezing on the superstructure. For three days and nights, we floundered in the Atlantic. Who could sleep? I could. With loose-fitting, navy-issue long johns, extra socks, my black watch cap, one mattress over and one under me, I slept like a bug in a rug.

Lemons to Lemonade
by Don Huling

OUR DAD WAS the kind of guy who could take a sour situation and make it into a barrel of fun—lemonade, if you please. Take the time one Christmas day in the early 1930s when he had to report for work while the entire plant was shut down for the winter. We had opened our gifts and finished our Christmas dinner. Dad announced that he had to go down to the Alpha Cement Company and carry the time clock for the 3:00 P.M. check.

"Would you boys like to come along?" he asked. John, Paul, and I rarely refused our dad when we got such invitations, because he usually made some kind of adventure or learning experience out of the occasion.

"Sure, Pop!" we all sounded off almost simultaneously. "Let's go!"

Carrying the time clock was an important function of protecting the plant and all the equipment inside it, we found out. The insurance company that had written the policy to cover any damage or vandalism while the plant was shut down

Alpha Cement Company headquarters building

demanded that someone responsible walk around the entire plant carrying a time clock that was punched with a key that had a number assigned to each station. In this manner a record was made of the time and station someone had visited. This was the job Dad had to do that Christmas day. A sour situation? Read on.

With his three boys in tow, Dad set off to make the rounds. We asked him what all those machines were for and what all those piles of white stone and black stone were. The first station was way out to the east end of the buildings. "This is where the limestone is brought in from the quarry and first crushed," he explained. "One day a stray dog fell into the crusher and guess what?" he said.

"Hamburger!" we all shouted.

"No," Dad said. "Believe it or not, that skinny dog went through the crusher without getting a bone broken. Tony took him home, fed him, and he is Tony's pet to this day. Sort of a wonder dog," Dad told us.

After the stone was crushed, it got pulverized. This is a very important step in making cement, but a very dusty operation back in those days. Since the plant was shut down there wasn't dust in the air, but it sure was thick on the floor. Dad's three boys had fun kicking up a real dust storm with the fine powder getting into our clothes and hair.

The pulverized stone is fed into one end of a large rotating kiln that is fired with coal dust. This giant piece of equipment lay at rest that Christmas day, but the way Dad explained it to us, we could almost see and feel the heat belching out of this sleeping dragon. Dad has a way of telling a story to his three boys that encouraged us to use our imaginations.

The burned stone was now called clinker and had turned black. This hot stone was put in a big pile to cool off before it

**Alpha Cement Company building
where 3 dusty boys took a shower**

was finally ground up with some shale to make cement. Dad took us down to the basement where Harry Noel worked testing briquettes made from the finished product. Harry wasn't working that day, but Dad explained how important it was to keep testing the product to make sure it was strong. There was one testing machine used to pull the briquettes apart to test for tensile strength. Cement isn't too strong when pulled apart, but in compression, Dad explained, it is hard to beat. That's why roads are built of cement.

We were getting sort of filled up with information, and Dad knew it was time to let his boys have some fun. After a hard day's work, the men at Alpha Cement were given time to wash up. That's what Dad thought would be fun for us boys. And he was right. Luckily there was hot water in the shower room even though the plant was shut down. We really had a good time getting all that cement dust off our faces and hands. Only one problem, however—we had a heck of a time getting all the cement out of our hair. We could hardly comb it.

Later on, when I was in high school, I had to do a science program for one of my teachers. I got some sample jars of stone from Dad and told the story of how cement is made at the plant where my dad worked. I got an A in this class. I remembered what Dad had told us that Christmas day when he turned a sour situation—lemons, if you will—into lemonade!

A Depression Christmas

SOON AFTER DAD died, I went through his desk drawers and found a letter that he'd had filed away since 1934. The letter was about hope. Hope, and Christmas.

Christmas day 1933 was cold and rainy. My family had exchanged our Christmas gifts, eaten our Christmas dinner, and gone to church, where Santa had presented each of us children with a lovely orange.

It was too miserable outside to play very long. Inside, the adults were quietly resting while we kids went to the play area of the basement. The centerpiece of the basement was the hand-fired coal furnace, which gave off enough heat to keep the basement quite warm. There was even a bed, which I remember sleeping on a few times, and hiding places, a Ping-Pong table, a workbench, and a game table.

There was a gentle knock on the back door just before the early winter darkness set in. I answered the knock to find a man standing in the cold. He asked if he could speak to the man of the house.

Dad came to the door, and the two men spoke for a few moments before Dad asked the man to step into the hallway. Dad left, spoke to Mom for a moment, then asked the man to follow him to the basement. My brothers and I listened in as we worked quietly on a model airplane on the other side of the furnace.

The man was hungry. Mom fixed him the same dinner we had enjoyed, while Dad talked to him and set up a table. The man told Dad he didn't want to impose on our Christmas; he just needed something to eat as he moved on his way. But Dad could see the man needed more.

He was a "bum"; that's what people generally called out-of-work men who were homeless. But there was something about this man that made the word "bum" seem out of place. It was obvious the man was well-educated but terribly down on his luck. He was far from home, lonely, desperate for work, and pretty dirty.

Dad provided soap and towels so the man could clean up before eating. He hung his outer clothes over a rack to dry by the warm furnace. The man's shoes were worn through and mushy with wetness. Dad threw them into the furnace, where they hissed and steamed for a long time before they finally burned.

Dad discovered that his good hunting boots were a perfect fit for the man. He gave the boots to him along with woolly socks he had stored in the basement armoire. You would have thought Dad had given the man $100.

The man talked about home and family, hundreds of miles away. He had left with the hope of finding work, but when he had reached his destination, there were no jobs, and he had no more money. Now he was walking and riding the rails, trying to go home. But he didn't know where each train he hopped would take him. He hunted for work in towns along the way. He had had a fine education, fine job, and a fine family—now he had nothing but hope to keep him going.

He and Dad talked for a long time. Then he left—clean,

dry, well-fed, and very appreciative of the help he had been given. None of us slept well that night as we thought of the man out in the cold with nothing but hope. I thought of his kids at home, not knowing where their dad was.

About a year later Dad and Mom read us a letter from the man who had come for Christmas. He was home. He had work. His family was OK.

He also said in the letter that the reason he turned in at our house as he was walking the streets looking for food was because there was a mark on the sidewalk, placed there by someone else, indicating that at this house you would not be turned away. I looked for the mark but never found it. It made me proud, though.

As I read the letter, soon after Dad's death, I recalled the story. In the letter, the man said he never lost hope because of people like Dad and Mom. "My feet stayed warm and dry all the way from La Salle, Illinois, to Iola, Kansas," he wrote.

The Lady Who Walked

I MIGHT NOT have remembered Saphronia except for my grandparents, who often discussed whether or not she would be visiting, and my father, who one day, not long after I was married, told my wife about knowing Saphronia while he was still a youth.

Saphronia was a gypsy lady whose son was incarcerated in Columbus, Ohio. As she had very little or no money, the trip to visit her son meant a long walk from Fort Wayne, Indiana, to Columbus and back, a round trip of more than three hundred miles.

I met Saphronia once when I was quite young. My family

was visiting my grandparents' farm near Carysville, Ohio, when my dad spotted Saphronia walking down the lane. She was wearing a black skirt that nearly reached the ground; it was quite dusty from walking along the gravel roads. On her head she wore a brightly colored shawl, which covered her graying black hair done up in a bun.

She looked different from anyone I had ever known. She carried a bag that looked like a bedroll in one hand and a walking stick in the other.

I thought Saphronia must have been one of my many relatives from the affectionate way Dad and Saphronia greeted one another. My grandparents also greeted her like family and invited her to dinner (dinner being the noon meal on the farm and supper being the evening meal).

The year I met Saphronia must have been about 1932. There was no electricity or radio on the farm, and my grandparents could not afford newspapers during the Depression. People like Saphronia were welcomed as valuable sources of news about what was happening along her route.

She described how the Depression was affecting farmers and families and brought word of births, deaths, and many other events between Fort Wayne and Columbus. Her mind must have been magnificent, to know what information to convey at each stop on her long journey.

During dinner, Saphronia captured the attention of everyone at the dining room table. After the meal my grandmother loaded a poke (a paper bag) with food so that Saphronia wouldn't go hungry before she reached the next friendly stopping point. My grandmother suspected that Saphronia fed others less fortunate than she was, as she walked along the roads and met many people who were looking for work or food.

Grandmother invited her to stop by on her return trip. After Saphronia failed to visit the farm, my grandparents wondered for many years what had happened. Had her son been released? Was she in poor health? Had the trip been too long for her to walk? These conversations kept me mindful of the woman who had walked and visited and made so many friends along the way.

I, too, have wondered why Saphronia's visits to the farm stopped. We don't know. But one thing I have never doubted is the love she had for her son.

PART II

TO THE FARM AND BACK

Don and Wilbur

Wilbur

ONE MORNING, ABOUT the year 1923, a frail small boy appeared at the kitchen door of my grandparents' farmhouse in central Ohio. He asked if he could cut the grass. One look told my grandparents that the boy had many problems: He looked too small to push a lawnmower. He appeared frightened, tired, and weak from hunger. Grandfather told him the grass was too wet to mow in the morning, but if he could hang around 'til after lunch, maybe he could give it a try. The boy stayed.

Grandfather never cut the grass again as long as he lived (1947). Wilbur Hart was his new "hired man." Hired men had their own bedrooms. Wilbur became part of the family.

Grandmother fed Wilbur some breakfast that first day, then dinner, then supper. She talked to him and found out that he was 14 years old (but looked about 9). His mother had died in Kentucky, he thought, and his father was a heavy drinker who never had a job. Wilbur and his father had walked from Kentucky to Ohio, going from farm to farm looking for work. This day Wilbur had set out on his own to support himself. Life had been no fun—so far—for Wilbur.

Wilbur had never been to school; he could not read or write. The only math he knew was that a penny was worth less than a dime, and a dime was worth two nickels. He had never had a dollar.

Grandmother taught Wilbur to read using a Montgomery Ward catalogue. That catalogue was a new, wonderful world to Wilbur. Of course, he had to learn about money before any of his dreams could come true, and he had to learn to write before he could place an order. Wilbur soon learned to count his money, save it, and study the catalogues.

He grew up a fine person.

My Train Ride to Conover

HOW I LOOKED forward to summertime when school would end! It meant I would pack my suitcase and get out of town as fast as I could to head for "The Farm." One year I was allowed to go by myself on the train. After letters back and forth between my parents and grandparents, a day was established that I would arrive at the train station in Conover, Ohio.

I went to the depot in La Salle long before the Rock Island Rocket was expected there. The stationmaster never smiled. He stood behind a raised frosted window, behind vertical bars of dull brass. One would transact business by slipping money for tickets under the bars, which ended a couple of inches above the worn countertop.

In the background of the ticket agent's office were three dirty windows: one facing east, one west, and one facing the train tracks. Just outside this window was a pole which signaled trains to do whatever the stationmaster commanded them to do. The signal had red and white arms that raised and lowered, plus colored lights.

The ticket agent room stank like old cigars and pipes. The floor was dirty, dusty, and the air around it musty smelling. The air was filled with clicking noises from the telegraph equipment located near the center window. The agent would often stop what he was doing, like looking up the routing and rate to Conover, and go click a message on the telegraph. I wondered how he could hear messages coming in while doing other things. Of course I imagined he was preventing a train wreck, saving hundreds of lives, if the incoming message was important enough for him to leave his searching for the route to Conover, Ohio.

STANDING: **Agnes, Alice, Thurman;** SITTING: **Grandpa John holding Paul, John, Grandma Jenny, and Don.**

The fare to Conover was about six dollars. I received two tickets, because I was going to transfer at Englewood, Illinois, to the Pennsylvania railroad.

The waiting room at my hometown depot was lit with dim lights, the walls were dingy, the squeaky wooden floor dusty and varnish-free, the benches hard, cold, and dirty. The men's washroom was such that I decided I didn't really need to use it. A sign stated: No Loitering.

Sometimes the ticket agent, stationmaster, signalman, and janitor—all the same man—would take off on a dead run down the flight of about thirty steps with a message. He attached this message to a pole that resembled a slingshot, the message centered in the string between the yokes. He would stand on the restricted side of the yellow line and hold the slingshot pole quite high in the air as a fast-moving steam train raced through town at about eighty miles per hour. People gasped with fear, stepping back ten or more feet from the yellow line as this man faced the oncoming train, which belched smoke, steam, dirt, dust, and soot. He stood firm, although he momentarily disappeared from view as the steam-spouting, thundering, screaming, hammering train came hurtling down the tracks.

Somewhere, hanging out of the cab of the engine, was the arm of a man. In a flash the crooked arm passed through the slingshot thing holding the note, and the note stayed in the crooked arm. I wondered how much the stationmaster got paid to stand closer to the train than the yellow line, especially after I saw suitcases left behind the line sucked under the fast trains, exploding the contents and spreading them for miles along the tracks. I believe he earned his wages.

Finally, waiting on the brick platform along the tracks, behind the yellow line, the baggage man (not the same man as the

Rock Island Depot, LaSalle

agent) rolled out a green wagon with red wheels. He tugged and pulled that wagon loaded with boxes and stuff to a predetermined spot along the tracks. Inevitably he arrived at that certain spot just as the Rocket blew its first audible blast announcing its arrival. Everybody immediately scurried up to the yellow line, trying to anticipate the exact spot where the Rocket would stop, so they could be first in line to climb aboard. The Rocket seldom stopped where the most people gathered.

The Rocket was silver with red trim, diesel powered. It bellowed hot, black exhaust from vents on top of the streamlined locomotive. On the front of the Rocket was a very, very bright light that swiveled back and forth, up and down, making the light shine a figure-eight pattern on the path ahead. In 1940 this was modern technology at its best.

The train conductor jumped off with a stool in one hand and his pocket watch in the other hand, thus giving the impression that if we didn't hurry saying good-byes and leap to board the train, he would signal the engineer to pull out and leave us behind. We hurried.

Inside the Rocket, it was quiet—quiet like being wrapped in a downy feather comforter. I could hear voices next to me, but those across the aisle were muffled into privacy. The seats were soft and comfortable, the engine hummed, the horns (not whistles) were barely heard and seemed to come from no direction at all. The Rocket was state-of-the-art in those good old days.

At the Englewood station, I disembarked and entered a cavernous, mausoleum-type train station. It was noisy, echoing every footstep, every cough; every loud voice was irritating, every voice added to the constant murmur. The loudspeaker barked train numbers, places they were going, and track numbers on which they would arrive, all in one blur of words that ran together as though spoken by a monotone who, when he saw a period coming up, dropped the already boring pitch to a dissonant lower tone on the last word. If he hadn't done that, no message would have had an ending.

I was a thirteen-year-old kid the first time I traveled alone, dragging my suitcase containing everything I'd wear for the next two and a half months. At Englewood I headed for the ticket counter to ask a ticket agent where I was supposed to go and how I would know if I got on the correct train. The answer was: "Look at the board up there!" The board didn't say Conover, Ohio; it didn't say if the train I wanted would be coming from the right or the left. It said things like: 9:21 A.M. Pittsburgh Track 7, 9:24 A.M. Denver Track 3, 9:51 A.M. New York Track 4.

So I watched people. I saw a man go up to the counter and ask for a schedule. The agent handed him a long narrow piece of cardboard. I looked around and found a discarded schedule on the floor; it listed places the train would go through. I went back and asked for a schedule to Conover, Ohio. The agent grabbed a card and shoved it at me. It said: Columbus, Ohio. I knew I was getting warm, and sure enough—in italics with a little star next to it—there was Conover, Ohio.

Back to the window again. I asked another agent whether the train to Columbus came from the left or from the right. He was a nice man; he said it would come from the right, would stop on Track 8, which was out "that" door, and should arrive in about ten minutes. He suggested I should tell the conductor as I got aboard to be sure to stop the train at Conover.

Getting aboard was a breeze. I was on my way.

The steam train to Ohio was not like the Rocket to Englewood. The seats were hard, covered with dark brownish mohair that griped like Velcro. (Rub it once with your hand, and your hand would be about the same shade of brown as the mohair.) The train took off with a series of bang, bang, bangs that grew louder with each bang, and when the bang got to my ear, luckily I was well-braced because the floor moved from under me at the time of the bang.

Leaving the Englewood Sixty-third Street station, the train moved very slowly as it sought out the right track to take it to Conover. Wheels squealed and squeaked as the car seemed to slip sideways, then ka-bang, ba-bang as the wheels apparently jumped some sort of gap at the rail crossing. This was repeated many times as the train drifted slowly through the maze of tracks at the switchyard, somewhere on Chicago's south side.

Finally it was time to sit back and try to relax as the train gained speed. I got accustomed to the constant jostling taking place between the train and the tracks. This was amplified through the hard seats.

I had fifty cents to spend for lunch, because train food was expensive. It was fun to try to walk the aisles to the dining car. I knew which way to go because I was on the last car. Entering the dining car, I was greeted by a black man in a starched white jacket, who led me to a table for four with a starched white tablecloth, pewter sugar bowl, creamer, and shakers, and a tall red rose in a skinny pewter holder. The napkin felt like cardboard, and the pewter tableware had a frosty silverlike appearance from constant jostling in the washbasin. Luckily I knew what a finger bowl was for.

It was hard to find something for fifty cents that would fill me up, but I did the best I could. I had to share my table with a nice lady, who pumped all the information from me that she possible could to keep conversation going. I enjoyed that and finally asked her where she was going and why. She responded that she was going home to be married and had just quit her job teaching school.

A schoolteacher? I ate lunch with a schoolteacher? A pretty one? One that wasn't old? What was this world coming to?

About halfway across Indiana, the ice that cooled the car a little bit was totally melted, so the car became hot. People opened windows, whose cracks were jammed with soot that drifted in over everyone and everything. I exited the car to the rear and stood on the platform, where there was a rail. I imagined myself standing there giving a whistle-stop speech.

Somewhere in Indiana, we stopped to get water for the steam engine and ice for cooling the cars. This was way out in the country. The icehouse was made of wet-looking, dark brown, unpainted wood. It had heavy doors like a refrigerator that were about a foot thick, and so were the walls. It made a lot of noise to load the ice, and the whole car shook as each block was shoved in under the car. We expected to be cool once again, but by now the summer heat was way ahead of the cooling effect of the ice. If the car ever cooled off again, it was after Conover, Ohio.

The conductor who had punched my ticket finally entered the car and yelled, "Conover next stop!" for all to hear. I expected he said it loudly to everyone because we would all get off there. But I was the only one.

Conover looked abandoned. There was no town, only a small railroad station surrounded by brick paving and a parking lot large enough for six autos. Only one automobile waited, and it belonged to Wilbur. He had given up an afternoon of farm work just for me! He had driven all the way from the farm—over fourteen miles—to pick me up for the summer. He asked me all about school, family, and myself. He told me all about the farm, what cowboy movies he would be taking me to that summer, and when the one hundred chickens would hatch at the St. Paris incubator.

I would raise them that summer. I would work to help my aging grandparents. Each year I would do more. School was out. I was on the farm. I was happy!

Billy the Workhorse

I'M NOT WHAT you would call a horsy person, but I've always liked horses.

My earliest memory of a horse was blind Mabel, my grandfather's old retired mare. She had worked for Grandpa all her life. She went blind before I was even born. She still wanted to work. She would pull the rope that lifted the hay into the loft of the barn. She loved to be spoken to and petted. That's what I did.

Billy, another horse, became my very special friend, however, when he saved my brother and me from a raging bull. The bull saw us picking blackberries, and although he was across the fence on the neighboring farm, he attacked

Thurman with buggy and Sorrel

The Old Buggy

In the old barn stands a buggy,
All covered with chaff and straw.
The wheels are bare of the rubber
That made it a pride and joy.

The shafts hang up in a corner
With the leather all brittle and
    gnawed.
It's a roost for some of the chickens,
Out of reach of the cats and the
    dog.

The cushion is turned over backward
With the edges all tattered and torn.
The hair makes a nest for the little
    mouse
That wants to keep cozy and warm.

The top that was made of leather
Has lost the luster and glow.
It has aged with the persons it
    sheltered
Not so many years ago.

The day was his eighteenth birthday
When the father spoke with ease,
"Son, take a look in the barn at your
    present
It's yours to use as you please."

It was covered with a piece of muslin
To keep it shining and new.
The odor of paint could be noticed
As he pulled back the cover to view.

us. Were we ever scared! John ran around a berry patch one way, and I went the other way as this charging, groaning bull tore up the earth trying to cut around the sharp curves. We had slowed his approach considerably, but quickly found ourselves in the pasture with no more bushes to circle, and the bull was still coming! And there stood Billy and Jerry, another of Grandpa's horses. Jerry was spooked easily, so he ran off when he saw us coming. I yelled whoa at Billy as John and I ran full speed and clambered onto his back. Billy just turned his head as we approached, then went back to eating grass with John and me sitting high aboard.

Once we were on Billy's back, the bull figured we had evaporated. He looked bewildered as he stamped around the berry bushes where he last saw us. Finally he gave up and started eating grass.

Now, Grandpa always trained his horses to obey voice commands. If you said whoa, they stopped; giddyap, they went forward; gee or haw, they turned left or right. So we sat on Billy, giving him voice commands till we got closer to another fence by the house. We gave Billy an ear of corn as a reward.

That was one day I'll never forget, but of Billy I have other memories, too. His sense of humor was amazing. After a long hard day's work, Wilbur would just want to put the horses out to pasture, but Billy wanted to play. Billy would pretend to eat grass when he

In a stall stood a lanky sorrel,
Her mane was a silvery gray.
She pawed and neighed as he
	entered the barn
As she wanted to be fed some hay.

She was hitched to the buggy in a
	hurry
With new harness and buckles bright.
The father and mother looked on with
	a smile
As he drove up the road out of sight.

Arrangements were made for a picnic
To be held along the river's shore.
The distance was far from the village
So the buggy had to carry four.

The day was warm and pleasant
And the cover fields scented the air.
The quartet sang as they rode along
In a world without a care.

When school days at home were
	forever gone
And the urge to go West hard to stave,
The rubber-tired buggy soon lost its
	charm
And the Sorrel went to her grave.

by Thurman H. Huling
November 4, 1943

should be on the way to the water trough. Wilbur would yell at him . . . then Billy would splash water on Wilbur if Wilbur were within ten feet of the water tank. Billy would rattle the tin cans that hung on the picket fence, then run off the opposite way from the pasture or run into the barn and stick his head out the door looking for Wilbur, waiting to be yelled at. Finally he'd charge off to the pasture where he would collapse onto the ground and roll in ecstasy, feet in the air, snorting. As Wilbur closed the gate, Billy would sit like a dog and whinny at him.

How could a horse that worked so hard be so happy?

Charlie

CHARLIE WASN'T BORN, he was hatched; at least that's the way I was told chickens came to be. My grandmother had found him in the grass between the house and the cow barn. He was alone. No hens had yet produced any chicks for the season. No hen in the barnyard acted the least bit interested in Charlie. Charlie wasn't peeping like he was lost, and he wasn't fearful of Grandmother when she picked him up. He was just alone and about one day old. He didn't seem to know he was a chicken; he thought he was something else, like maybe just a small person.

Grandmother wrapped him in an old sock and put him in a shoebox in the corner of the kitchen. She really expected him to die before I arrived the next day to spend my summer on the farm.

But Charlie didn't die. I coaxed him to eat oatmeal from my hand and let him walk around in a saucer of water until he figured out he didn't like water except to drink. He was always busy, never seemed lonesome (although I did visit him quite often), and he loved his box and sock.

Charlie soon became the kitchen floor crumb picker-upper; however, he required close follow-up. He spent his days in the fenced-in yard around the house. No other chickens were ever

Gramp Huling and chicken Charlie

allowed in the yard, only Charlie. But Charlie was an outcast. If he ventured into the barn lot, the large chickens attacked him.

When the other chicks hatched from the incubator, Charlie was too large to fit in with them, so he continued to live alone in his shoebox in the kitchen.

One evening, after chores were done, I went to a movie in St. Paris. It was a big deal for me to be taken to a movie, and I forgot to find Charlie and put him to bed. At sundown my grandmother heard and saw Charlie outside her bedroom window looking for her. She had often talked to Charlie from her bedroom as she rested, but this night he had come to deliver a message! By the time Grandmother got to the kitchen door to retrieve him, Charlie was already there. When she opened the door, he popped right in and ran, head down, straight to the shoebox!

From then on, Charlie watched the back door at sundown. If it closed he would fly up and bump the screen door, and if that didn't work he would head for Grandmother's bedroom window. It soon became a game between the two of them.

As he got older—that is, a few weeks older—he began roosting on the shoebox, on my lap, on my shoulder, on a chair, anyplace at bedtime. He couldn't figure out why his shoebox had grown so small that it wouldn't hold him up anymore. He'd jump into his box, jump out, then jump right back in where he felt secure. It was time to train Charlie to roost with the rest of the flock.

So after dark one night I took Charlie from his secure little box and placed him on a roost in the chicken coop with the older chickens. The next morning, when I let the chickens out of the coop, Charlie didn't come out. I found him on a back roost, all alone. He had overslept!

As Charlie grew into a rooster, he would not fight. I

wondered about that as I left the farm at the end of the summer. I also wondered if he would still be tame and such a unique individual when I returned the next summer.

I shouldn't have worried about Charlie. When I returned the next year, I immediately asked about him. Wilbur said Charlie was still around someplace and if I found him I should try to figure out what to do with him. I wondered if something was wrong. . . .

To locate Charlie I took two coffee cans and beat them together. All the chickens I had raised the year before came running from every direction. They had forgotten why they should run to me—now a stranger to them—but here they came! I had used this method to call them at feeding time when they were chicks. Charlie was easy for me to spot because he came right up to me to check out my pants cuffs for anything good to eat. The rest of the chickens wandered off with a bewildered look about them, but one hen stayed with Charlie. That's when I found out. . . .

Charlie was monogamous. He had one friend and that was enough. He wouldn't fight, didn't have a territory, didn't have a harem, didn't carouse; he was "different." So I told Wilbur that Charlie was smart. . . . If he had acted like the rest of the roosters he probably would have been Sunday dinner a long time ago.

Charlie proved he was smart in other ways, too. He followed Grandpa around, sat with him, roosted on him, and just generally knew Grandpa was good for cuff picking. I saw Grandpa "spill" corn into his cuffs a few times that summer. They were great friends.

The next few years I missed going to the farm, but when I finally did go, there was old Charlie, less tame, but just as smart. Looked like a young hen was with him, though. . . .

BB Guns

DAD BOUGHT DON AND JOHN BB guns one Christmas. At the time, I was too young to have one, and two were plenty anyway. They cost $1.25 each: Daisy, single-shot—a good way to learn gun safety and to target-practice under the very close supervision of Dad. It wasn't long before I could hit the paper the target was printed on, while Don was hitting the target and John was hitting the bulls-eye. I never forgot the things Dad taught us about safety. Actually, I feared all guns and still do. Mom sent the BB guns, with us boys, to our grandparents farm and made sure the guns stayed there. A good move.

One day at the farm, Uncle Charlie came to visit. He was impressed by the seriousness with which John handled his BB gun and sort of made fun of John for the way he handled a mere toy, as Uncle Charlie called it.

It's not a toy, Uncle Charlie, it's a gun that can kill things, John told his uncle.

So Uncle Charlie took a walk with John to the orchard near the house, where a rabbit hopped out of the tall grass. Bet you can't even scare it, said Uncle Charlie.

The rabbit hopped a few feet away and stopped to look back. It was about forty feet away. John quickly raised the BB gun and fired. The rabbit dropped dead! John had hit it in the eye.

Uncle Charlie was in deep trouble with Grandma for encouraging John to shoot animals. She made Uncle Charlie take the rabbit home for Aunt Silvia to cook, which he did, but forevermore he told the story about John, the sharp-shooter, until it became legendary in the area. Uncle Charlie embellished it more each year.

Wilbur was a true sportsman. His sport was hunting. His choice of rifle was a single-shot .22 short. That is the first step above a BB gun. Wilbur loved to stalk his prey. He disliked rifles that had more than one bullet. To him it was no sport to be able to rapid-fire. One chance is all he wanted. If he missed, the prey escaped. That was fair. His choice was hunting groundhogs, and he hunted them because of the holes they dug that could break a horse's leg and the crops they destroyed. He might hunt all day and never fire a shot. It wasn't that he didn't see anything; it would be because the one shot he was limited to had to be exactly right or he wouldn't take it. Often he would return from a day of hunting and tell us about the things he saw but didn't shoot at. During the Depression years, Wilbur helped keep food on the table, but he would rarely shoot a female squirrel or pheasant or quail.

My Huling grandparents were really hard hit during the Depression. The price of corn they had raised to sell was so low they couldn't afford coal, so they burned corn to heat and cook. Coal was worth more than corn. On a wall in their barn was nailed a collection of license plates—missing were the Depression years.

My Return to City Life

SUMMER ALWAYS ENDED. Back home in Illinois, it was supposed to feel good to sleep late, but I couldn't. I thought about my grandpa getting up with the first crowing rooster and heading for the well to pump a tin cup of water before carrying the shiny milk pails to the barn.

And I wouldn't be there to milk Big Red, the cow I had milked twice each day all summer. I wouldn't be there to pump the cold well water for the milk house, either. Well water was what we used to cool the milk after we had filtered it into large Sidney Dairy milk cans.

It was nearly time for me to start school again, but I would miss the farm. I'd miss my chickens, too. My grand-mother had said that I had done very well to raise so many of the one hundred day-old chicks I had started with.

Each evening during my last week at the farm, I had carried each chicken to the coop and placed it on a roost with the older chickens. I had done that enough times so that they now retired each sundown to the coop instead of to the crowded box where I had raised them.

And my grandmother would have to gather the eggs her-self, while I sat in a classroom worrying that she might not find the eggs in the empty stall of the horse barn.

I would be missed. I knew I would.

When I had arrived home after being on the farm all summer, I hardly knew my family. It seemed they had changed. The girls were less giggly and acted very grown-up—"mature," they called it. The boys had all grown big feet and much taller. My best friend, Ezzie, had grown a foot, I think. Why, he was as tall as me now, even though I had grown taller, too. My older brothers were dating girls! And my sister, the oldest of the four of us, had a boyfriend who drove all the way from Ohio to Illinois in a nice, new 1940 La Salle automobile.

He brought my sister a gift, a windup record player. And he brought me a BB gun. I was impressed. But Sis hedged on that boyfriend. She didn't marry him.

It was time for me to take on more responsibility, so I took over Don's paper route while he got jobs that paid more.

I soon discovered that my paper route customers had personalities similar to those of the chickens I had raised over the summer. Some were prompt when I collected the fifteen cents due each week, and some were slow. Some were quite forgetful. Some were friendly and wanted to talk. And some were sort of like the young roosters I had just raised, in that they wanted to crow a lot. But in general, my customers treated me well.

I quickly got back into the routines of living the city life. But I sure missed the farm as autumn began. Maybe next summer I can drive the team of horses as we make hay. . . .

A Trip to Remember

FOR SOME REASON, the year 1934 was a good enough year for the farm to produce enough profit for Wilbur to drive us three brothers to Illinois and attend the World's Fair in Chicago as part of his trip.

Wilbur owned a 1929 Ford Model A roadster, without a rumble seat. It was a simple machine. If it got cold, side curtains were installed to keep out the cold. If it rained, side curtains were installed to keep out the rain. Side curtains were the only accessory the car came with, but Wilbur added wing windows to help deflect some of the cold wind or rain.

The Model A had one seat. I was the smallest of the three boys, so I sat on a little stool used for milking cows, on the floor in front of my big brothers Don and John. It was comfortable until we got to maybe Piqua, Ohio, about sixteen miles from the farm. The trip was over three hundred miles long. We left the farm in the morning darkness and arrived in La Salle long after the sun set, about fourteen hours later (average speed about twenty-five miles per hour).

I don't know how Wilbur stood having us all the way to Illinois, but we boys had great respect for Wilbur. Besides giving us movie reviews in wonderfully humorous detail, he could roll his own cigarettes as he drove his roadster down the road and always had one hand on the steering wheel as he did it.

I must digress for the sake of my grandchildren to explain roll-your-own cigarettes. Wilbur smoked Bull-Durham cigarettes. Bull-Durham tobacco came in a white cotton pouch about the size of a pack of cigarettes. The pouch had two orange-colored drawstrings; as you pulled them apart, the top of the pouch closed. To one of the drawstrings was attached a piece of thin cardboard about the size of a nickel, very important. To the side of the pouch was an orange packet of cigarette paper, very thin. Each thin paper had a lick-glue edge. The idea was to blow on the papers' edges until one sheet was isolated from the rest, then remove it, holding it between two fingers lengthwise to keep it from bending in the middle. Next, the pouch was opened by spreading the top open; this took two hands, or teeth and one hand. Then tobacco was carefully poured onto the cigarette paper while holding it in a V or U shape lengthwise. Now the tobacco had to be spread, but first the pouch had to be closed and put back into one's pocket. This is where the little cardboard tag came in handy. The tag was easy to bite, and the orange string could be pulled with fingers, thus closing the pouch with one hand.

Now it was time to spread the tobacco over the length of the paper and lick the glued edge. Rolling the paper and tobacco between the index and forefinger made the cigarette. To keep tobacco from falling out the tip of the cigarette one would light, it was pinched and rolled to a point, while the other end went in the mouth. Everything was ready now.

Lighting was the next objective. Farmers like Wilbur carried stick matches in a can that had once contained bouillon cubes. The can was about the length of a cigarette and about three-quarters of an inch in diameter. The can kept the

Grandma Hawthorne

matches dry. Wilbur would strike the match on the thigh of his Montgomery Ward overall pants (later known as blue jeans) and light his cigarette all in one motion.

Now back to the fact that Wilbur could do all this in a roadster and keep one hand on the steering wheel at the same time! Much later in life, I proved to my friends that I could roll my own cigarette, using both hands, in a quiet place, but I could not stand the strong tobacco of Bull-Durham; it took some kind of man to smoke that stuff! But hey, it only cost a nickel a pouch, which would easily make twenty or more cigarettes. A lot of Bull-Durham was sold during the Depression.

In the heat of the afternoon, we stopped at one of the many farms that had red juice for sale. We never knew what the red juice was, but for years as we traveled with our parents, we had wanted to stop and enjoy a nice cold drink of red juice. So Wilbur stopped. The juice not only tasted real bad, it was hot. So we drove on. I slept on my brothers' laps.

When we arrived in La Salle, my parents and my grandmother on my mother's side were happy to greet us with dinner they had prepared and saved for us. I don't remember much about the dinner, but Wilbur did, for years and years. Wilbur loved to tell my grandparents on the Huling side, where he lived, about my grandmother from Kansas who was visiting Illinois. He would tell about the scalding-hot, watery soup she carefully placed in front of him, and Wilbur, who would normally blow on the spoon and slurp such hot things, sat quietly and patiently for the soup to cool. Just as he was ready to partake of the somewhat cooler soup, my grandmother came and snatched it away, thinking he was finished.

Now my Grandmother Hawthorne was a prim and proper woman whose job it was to be a housemother at a college fraternity. She taught her boys manners, judging from the attempts she made at helping my mother raise three boys born within a three-year period. We loved her when she visited, but thought at the time we would never measure up to her standards of what gentlemen should be.

Well, Wilbur apparently went through hell at mealtime, thinking my grandmother was out to either starve him or poison him. Wilbur drank coffee, but Grandmother never allowed the coffeepot to be at the table. The pretty teapot was always there, but never an ugly coffeepot. So, unless my grandmother offered Wilbur more terribly weak coffee, Wilbur had but one cup—which, by the way, he drank while it was too hot for fear she would snatch it up from in front of him and carry it off. Wilbur didn't care for Kansas cooking.

He also loved to tell about how my Grandmother Hawthorne set out "all the silverware in the house" for each meal. Spoons that weren't needed! Forks of every shape when only one was needed! And salads fed him like he was a rabbit, not a farmer. Wilbur never said so, but I don't think he liked my Grandmother Hawthorne much.

So off Wilbur went to the World's Fair of Chicago. While he was there he bought a brand-new set of Firestone tires for his Model A. How proud he was to show my dad that the inner tubes in his new tires were "gum-dipped."

Thirty years later, those gum-dipped inner tubes were in such good shape I stretched them from twenty-one to thirty-two inches and installed them on a Stanley Steamer that had broken down in front of the farm in Ohio.

The trip to Illinois was the longest trip Wilbur had ever made. For years he talked about every little town we drove through and the details of each town that the rest of us had never noticed or paid any attention to. It was a big world out there, and Wilbur was quite content to remain in his small area. He used to wonder how folks from the city could stand not having a woods nearby where they could sit under a big tree and watch the squirrels, other animals, and birds.

A Second Chance

FRED SCHMOEGER AND I were friends—not close, but neighborhood kids together. He lived at the corner of Eighth and Gooding Streets. We both attended Lincoln School in La Salle. I was in second grade that year, and Fred, who was small for his age, was in sixth grade.

Fred Schmoeger

One day we got to horsing around at the chinning bar on the playground during recess. We pushed each other off the bar and tussled. We weren't fighting, just playing rough.

The principal, Miss Moran, was on recess duty. She spotted us. She tolerated no rough activities while she was on duty. Neither Fred nor I thought we were misbehaving, but she "clanked" her bell to get our attention.

We stopped our "fight," as she called it, as she approached us. She looked sternly at both of us and then said she'd see us after recess.

What fear entered my heart! I must have been ghost-white. Fred was also gulping for air as Miss Moran resumed her slow walk around the schoolyard.

"Do you think she'll forget?" I asked Fred.

"She never forgets," he replied.

Sure enough, after recess, there was a knock on the door

of my second-grade classroom. It was Miss Moran. She had come to call me out of class.

As I left the room, I couldn't look to the left or the right. My eyes were on the floor as though I were counting the floorboards.

Out in the hall stood Miss Moran. She looked to be nine feet tall, while Fred, standing beside her, looked mere inches tall. What punishment will I receive? I wondered as I approached fearfully.

Then I saw it! Miss Moran had brought her large, wide ruler, the one she used to administer punishment.

Oh, what fear possessed me at that moment!

Standing before us, she asked us what we thought we had been doing on the playground of her school. Did we think we were going to get away with that kind of activity? We just stood there, shaking—our heads especially, but also the rest of our bodies.

Fred and I both told her we were friends. We had only been playing rough, we explained, and had not intended to let the situation get out of hand. That was the truth.

Miss Moran lectured us sternly for a long time while she made up her mind whether or not to believe us. As she stood there talking, she kept whacking her large ruler against the palm of her left hand.

At each crack of the ruler against her palm, we jumped with fear, convinced that we would be next to feel its agony.

Fortunately for us, we somehow convinced her that we had indeed been just horsing around. We promised Miss Moran to play without roughhousing from that moment on.

And we kept our promise.

Miss Moran was my teacher when I reached eighth grade. She became my favorite teacher in grade school, because she encouraged underachievers to come out of their shells and develop their strengths to the utmost of their abilities.

That year I was in second grade had been her first year as principal of Lincoln School. By the time I reached eighth grade, she had either mellowed or had sufficiently conveyed her authority to the point that she was able to put away her ruler—and the children behaved in a socially acceptable manner.

Maybe Fred and I had a lot to do with the behavior of the kids at Lincoln School. We were famous during our remaining years there as the first students to convince Miss Moran that we really could behave if given a second chance.

One Note

WHEN I WAS a little boy, the church I went to had a children's choir. We practiced every Thursday afternoon after school. We would meet at the church and practice a song until we knew it well enough to sing it for the grownups in church on a Sunday or some special day like Christmas.

There was one boy in the choir who sang only one note.

Strawn Gay

Most of us could sing pretty well, but Strawn showed up every Thursday for practice and joined us, singing his one note.

Some of the kids tried to tell him he couldn't sing, but Strawn came to practice anyway and sang in church with the rest of us. Sometimes we'd tease Strawn by telling him to sing real loud because sometimes the note he sang was the right note and we would sound real good when we got to "Strawn's note."

Then one day we sang a very difficult song in church. We had practiced a long time on this song, and there was one part at the end of the song where we were supposed to sing real loud. No matter how loudly we sang this part of the song, Mrs. Bett, the choir director, would open her mouth wide and shake her hands in the air, trying to get us to sing louder!

That Sunday, the first note Mrs. Bett wanted us to sing louder was "Strawn's note." He sang his one note so loudly, the rest of us were amazed. It was a long note; we seemed to hold it an awfully long time. And what would we do on the next note? If Strawn sang the first note that loud and the next note he sang was going to be the same note while the rest of us sang a different note, we'd better sing very loud to drown him out. So we tried.

But on the next note, Strawn sang the right note with us, and the next, and the next notes he sang with the rest of us, the right notes, loud! How wonderful! We all shouted out our notes. Poor Mrs. Bett almost fainted.

When we were finished singing, all the kids in the choir were looking at Strawn with our mouths open. After church we told him he had a good voice. We asked him what had happened; he had never sung before.

Strawn told us he could sing, but he could only sing real loud, not softly like the rest of us, so he usually sang his one note softly.

From then on, each time the children's choir sang, Mrs. Bett would make sure there was a place where she could wave her arms and shake her hands at us to get us to sing loudly. When Strawn sang out, so did we; he inspired us.

Congregational Church Choir, Easter, 1938. See page 253 for names.

We told Strawn to sing all the time, that it was OK if he was louder than the rest of us, but Strawn never did. He only sang out when everybody else did.

Strawn taught us a lesson: God had given Strawn the talent to sing loud. He couldn't sing softly, but when he could use his talent he did! We wished we'd known he had that talent all along and had looked for ways for him to use it.

Each of us has talents that don't always show up right away. Sometimes it takes years for us to find all of our talents. We go along doing something, feeling we don't really fit in with everyone else, then all of a sudden we are inspired to let the world know we can do it!

Talents are gifts from God.

✳   ✳   ✳

High-Cuts and Christmas Stamps

THE ILLINOIS WEATHER was brutal the winter of 1936. It was so snowy I actually talked my parents into buying me high-cuts, leather boots that laced up almost to the knee. I thought I was ready for anything with high-cuts, only to find out they weren't good at keeping the feet warm when the temperature was near zero.

But weather didn't matter—I was in style! Why, I could wade through snowdrifts as deep as my waist and not get snow in my boots. I was ready for anything that winter could throw at me—except cold.

One of my friends, Logan, also had high-cuts. We would leave his house after school to make trails in the snow where no one else had trod. Then it quit snowing and turned cold.

One day Logan read in a magazine about a wonderful offer to earn a BB gun by selling Christmas seals. Christmas seals were sheets of paper stamps with glue on the back that one would lick, then stick on a gift to hold the wrapping paper. On the front were punch-out pictures of Santa Claus, holly wreaths, snow-covered houses, and decorated Christmas trees. Some stamps were printed

High-cuts

"Merry Christmas and Happy New Year," and a few, just a few, said: "To: _____ From: _____," the idea being that if one wanted enough To and From stamps for a family, one had to buy more than one packet of stamps.

I offered to help Logan sell, so he ordered them. Of course, his folks had to pay for them in advance, and he would have to sell hundreds of packets of seals to earn an item as valuable as a brand-new BB gun. Part of the deal was that for every ten packets of seals sold, he would earn a dime, while still earning the BB gun if he sold them all.

Logan could have given away all the packets of stamps and still claimed the gun, but the price of the stamps would have been two or three times more than the gun was worth. So Logan was really put to the test. If he wanted to earn the BB gun and make money, he had to get out and sell.

I had experience knocking on doors, because I helped my brother Don collect from his paper route customers each Saturday morning. I knew that one must approach each house using the sidewalks, climb the front porch steps without stomping one's feet but making a goodly amount of noise, then rap on the door without pounding. If there was a doorbell, one must use it first, then wait. The rule was never knock or ring more than three times.

Logan and I set out with high hopes of selling all his Christmas stickers in the section of town where we thought most people had been employed during those Depression years. We quickly learned that the stamps issued by the March of Dimes for the Tuberculosis Foundation supported by President Roosevelt were the preferred choice for people who could afford them.

Eventually we found a very good approach. No matter who answered the door, we would ask to speak with "the lady of the house." That was quite a catchy phrase, because if it was a man who answered the door he immediately knew we weren't there to confess we had broken something or to ask the kids of the house to come out and play. If a woman answered the door, she was flattered to be called "the lady of the house."

The lady of the house was usually preparing dinner for the family, so we would jump right in with our sales pitch and explain to the man that we were selling Christmas seals for only a dime a pack in order to earn a prize. Rather than bother his wife, the man would gladly purchase at least one package of stamps. Sometimes we'd sell him more when we pointed out that there weren't many To and From stickers in each package.

Dinnertime was the best selling time. When the door opened, we would give a little shiver and appear to look like waifs who had been out in the cold for a long time. We sold a lot of stamps.

We never stayed out until we were late for our own suppers, and we never went out after supper.

Logan earned his BB gun. He was well trained by his father in its proper use. It was never loaded unless he was using it, and he never, ever, used it in my presence. He understood, as did his parents, brother, and sister, it was not a toy.

By the time spring arrived, my high-cuts were not much good. They had been soaked so often they were stiff and curled up at the toes. I also had outgrown them. It felt mighty good to replace those heavy high-cuts with summer tennis shoes and not have to mess with all those laces. The next winter I wore galoshes.

Headline: "Huling No-Hitter"

IN 1991 THE BIG NEWS in baseball was that Nolan Ryan pitched his seventh no-hitter. My brother John only pitched one no-hitter, but it was worth seven times seven.

John spent his year of sixth grade in bed with rheumatic fever. He didn't do well; it left his heart damaged. The following year he spent away from the city, with our grandparents on their farm. There he regained his strength to the point that he seemed normal. But he had learned his limits: when he would tire, he would rest; he would pace himself during extended activities; he was careful.

John and I used to play catch lot. It was a good way to play together without him getting too worked up. John could pace his endurance this way.

Then one morning up at Hegeler Park, one of the two teams that showed up was missing their pitcher. They were about to forfeit the game when John approached the team captain and said he would pitch for them. So what if they lost the game; with him they would have nine men and could at least play ball that day. Somehow John convinced them he could pitch. He had never pitched a game before in his life.

About the fourth inning word got to me that my brother was pitching a no-hitter. Three up and three down. This I had to see. I headed my bike to the ball diamond.

About the sixth inning the local newspaper's sports writer quietly slipped into the bleachers, which were filling up. Who told him, we'll never know. I think he just sensed it.

Now, this was not Little League; it was "limited organizational." Teams of friends were made up by a captain, not a parent. Coaching was among the team members. There were no linemen, no referees. The umpire, John Strell, was the one and only person employed by the city to see that ball games didn't end in riots and that the two teams who signed up to play got first crack at the field. The umpire was also a favorite amongst the kids because of his honesty and integrity.

Well, John went all the way—no hits, no runs. He came home and went to bed. I worried, but kept quiet so Mom and Dad wouldn't know why he was resting. He wasn't supposed to play baseball, yet our folks knew he could never live under glass, so they became more concerned that he know his limits rather than try to restrict his activities.

That afternoon, as I was folding my newspapers for delivery, I saw it in the paper: "NO-HITTER AT PARK TODAY." Of course, Mom and Dad read it, too. They had a talk with John. He assured them he would quit while he had a perfect record.

Dad asked, "How did you do it?" with pride in his voice.

John said, "I knew if they hit the ball I'd have more balls to throw!"

Tar

ONE DAY, WHEN I was about ten, my friends and I noticed a smell in the air and dark clouds of smoke emanating from a huge black contraption. It was a tar machine! One man kept the fire roaring under a barrel-shaped pot, while other men filled sprinkling cans with the boiling hot stuff, which they carried off to pour on a roof or on some driveway cracks that needed filling.

The tar machine made lots of noise, like a steam engine getting ready to pull a heavy load. Wow! We were impressed! The tar machine operator wore bib overalls that were almost so stiff with splashes of hardened tar that they could stand by themselves if he weren't in them.

"Say, boys," he called, "ever chew warm tar?"

We looked at each other and laughed. Of course we had never chewed warm tar! Who in the world would chew that stuff?

"Here's how you do it," he said as he took a small patch off a warm spot on his machine. "First you make sure it's not too hot, then you roll it around in your hands to make a ball. Then you chew it. It makes your teeth real white, see?"

He grinned a toothy grin as he placed the black ball in his mouth and began chewing. His teeth didn't look exceptionally white at the time.

"Here, take some," he said, handing us little balls of the warm stuff. So we carefully followed his directions and began to chew. Of course we spit a lot; it didn't taste like anything good to eat, and besides, he spit a lot, too.

So off we went, chewing our tar. It wasn't long before the tar cooled to body temperature and was extremely difficult to chew. We figured that it was cleaning our teeth quite well when that happened. Finally, it was too much, and our tired jaws demanded relief, so we threw it out.

On our way home, we passed the tar machine again, and the man yelled out, "Where's your chews? You didn't throw them out, did you? All you have to do is lay 'em in the sun awhile, and they'll soften right up! Here, have some more for later."

So we got more. This was hotter than the first batch, almost runny, and one had to quickly change it from hand to hand because it felt like it would burn.

"That'll really be good in a minute," he said as he crossed the street with a shovel. There he scooped up a dead cat that had been killed by a car and when he returned, he threw the carcass into the boiling black mass.

"That adds flavor," he shouted over the roar of the tar machine. "Third one I've found today!"

So please don't offer me tar to chew . . . I prefer other ways to clean my teeth.

A Hot Summer Hike

IT WAS TOO hot in town, so the older boys from the neighborhood decided to walk the towpath along the old abandoned Illinois and Michigan Canal. Being the youngest member of the group of boys, I was delighted to tag along. The year must have been about 1938.

The walk to Split Rock was cool and refreshing compared to the heat building up in town. The name Split Rock came about when the canal was built, because of a huge boulder that had to be cut through to complete the canal. Split Rock was about halfway to Utica.

The I&M Canal was not in operation for very long before railroads took over. At Split Rock there was not enough space for train tracks, canal, and the towpath, so the railroads cut a tunnel through half of the split rock. It was fun to watch steam trains leave the tunnel and to see the black smoke shoot in the air as the train exited. It was dangerous to walk through the tunnel, as trains didn't slow down and

Split Rock

there was precious little space between the rail cars and the soot-covered walls.

Rock Island workers cut a tunnel through Split Rock on the north bank to lay a second set of tracks. A bridge was built over the tunnel, and a trestle supporting railroad tracks between the two remaining portions of Split Rock was built over the I&M Canal. The tracks carried CO&P (Chicago, Ottawa, and Peoria) electric-powered cars, a popular form of transportation competing for passenger traffic in the early decades of the 1900s. The canal passenger packets ended about five years after the opening of the canal due to railroad competition. However, cargo boats continued to use the canal for over sixty years.

First we climbed Split Rock, using a cable someone had fastened near the top of the rock. From up there one could see the Illinois River and the wide valley it formed. Then we ate the lunches we had brought along for the outing.

One of the older boys suggested we visit the caves nearby. The caves were part of an abandoned silica sand mine. The mining of sand was dangerous and no longer profitable with the advent of strip mining.

We found the caves were full of bats hanging from the ceilings. If one pokes a sleeping bat, it flies around crazily and makes screaming noises. It wasn't long before the bats, thousands of them, drove us out of the caves. One look at their ugly faces and teeth and I was long gone from the cave I was in. I never bothered a bat again.

There was but one thing left to explore and that was the abandoned silica mill, where the sand from the caves had been processed and stored in bins that were nearly as tall as cement mill silos.

On the way, we came upon a small brick structure that resembled an outhouse, but it had clear cold water running from under the door. The door was not locked, so we went in. We found a pipe extending from the stone wall behind the building, from which water flowed, causing the stream of water under the door. To us it was ice-cold, that hot day, so we refilled our canteens, drank, and splashed each other just to hear the screams as the cold shock hit hot bodies. My wise brother Don told me not to drink any more than I already had because it might not be safe.

Then we moved on to the silos, or storage rooms, full of silica sand. The buildings looked safe as they were made of brick and large barn beams. There wasn't much to see from the ground, so we climbed the ladders that went to the tops of the bins. Much to our surprise, there was sand in most of the bins and there were ladders inside the bins in case anyone inside wanted to climb out.

One of the boys jumped into a bin of sand from about ten feet of height. He sank so deep when he landed that he had a hard time trying to get to the ladder. So he lay on his belly and wiggled over to it. That was good enough; most all the older boys jumped in.

When they got out of the bin, they were snow-white all over their bodies—hair, shoes, pants, shirts, faces, and arms. The solution was to throw the clothes in the creek, wash them, and hang them out in the sun to dry, returning to the mill in the nude.

Each bin was more daring than the last because the jump to the sand was a longer distance and one would sink in further. Then there were sand-sprinkling contests to see whose body would hold the thickest layer of sand before it fell off. As the afternoon wore on, the old building grew hotter and hotter, and our sweaty bodies began to tire, so we finally gave up playing to head for home.

But first we washed up in the spring. I learned that day, if one sticks his head in ice-cold water after being very hot, one gets an extreme headache!

At the dinner table that evening, my dad asked his three sons how our hike had gone. So we gave him all the details of the day. When we were finished, he asked us if we had ever heard of silicosis. Of course we had not. So he explained how fine silica dust filled the lungs of workers, causing them to be disabled. He went into more detail, then suggested (in such a way that it really hit home to all three of his sons) that we could have been arrested, could have had thermal shock, could have been buried in sand flow, could have fallen from great heights, could have drunk polluted water, etc.

I might have forgotten that hike except for the lessons my dad gave us on our return. We never went back, and a few months later, the old mill was torn down.

A few years after that, the old silica mill site was in the news: found in the caves there was a still for making whiskey from local corn. The water came from the spring. I wondered if the bootleggers ever had the water tested. Apparently it didn't matter, because they used horse urine to give the whiskey color.

Halloween

BEING THE YOUNGEST of three brothers meant I was sometimes left out of the projects my brothers dreamt up. It was usually my oldest brother, three years my senior, who planned the schemes, and his siblings were followers. Thus was the case one Halloween night. I was an observer, not a partaker for some reason, I'm happy to say.

The year was about 1937, which made me ten years old.

As Halloween was all tricks and no treats in those days, I imagine I was not in on this event because I couldn't run fast enough, or wouldn't keep my mouth shut if suspicion of the incident came my way.

The plan was this: our neighbor had a single wire fence, about a foot high, around his backyard. The purpose was to prevent us kids from making a path to get to the alley where we played. The fence caused us to make a path through another neighbor's backyard. The wire was stiff, about an eighth of an inch in diameter, which made it very strong. The idea was to take down the fence and use the wire in a different undisclosed location where it was not expected to be.

Because there was no way the wire could be cut by any tools available in the darkness of night, my brothers just took the entire length of wire, about eighty feet. It was hard to handle, being quite stiff, so it needed to be anchored at each end if its purpose was to be to trip someone up by, say, stringing it about six inches off the ground between trees, where someone would walk that Halloween night.

It was then that the new plan was born. Why not string it across the street, in front of our house, from one elm tree on our side to an elm directly on the other side? It would need to be raised up to maybe thirty inches in height, and something would have to be hung on the wire to alert the driver of any auto that came along so the car could stop in time. It would be quite funny to watch motorists come to a stop and then have to back up the street to detour around the block.

The wire worked perfectly; it was long enough to meet itself and be twisted into a splice that would hold quite nicely. But it sagged in the middle, so a brother found a two-by-four and halfway across the street wound it round and round, like a tourniquet. To keep it from unwinding he wedged it into the bricks that paved the street. The show was about to begin.

The best view was from my parents' bedroom window, so that's where they observed what took place next. Down the street rolled a 1936 Ford, quite new. The driver didn't see the two-by-four standing in the middle of the street until it was too late. Even one-year-old Fords couldn't stop very quickly in those days, but the driver slowed a little—very little—till he hit the wire. At the wire all forward motion stopped suddenly for that Ford! The two-by-four came loose from the bricks and spun around, bashing the top of the hood; the double strand of tightly wound wire held firm as it cut into the grille and front fenders of the car, shearing off the fender-mounted headlights.

I believe my brothers sensed they could be in trouble at this point because later on they whispered back and forth between each other about something I would later find out anyway.

The man took his Ford to the police station.

Next morning Dad got a phone call to stop by.

By noon the event was ended. The fence was reinstalled in the neighbor's yard, although it never looked the same. (It had wrinkles from one end to the other.)

Here was a man, the man who hit the wire, who thought my brothers had talent! What a fantastic trick to pull off on Halloween! He took it as a prank, saying he had done things almost that bad when he was younger and had been let go with a lesson well learned. He did not press charges, did not make my dad or brothers pay for damages. Wow! What a nice guy!

Dad had a talk that afternoon with all three of his boys, just in case I had any ideas of my own about pulling off a prank on anyone.

Troop 2 Camps Out

THE BIG EVENT of the year was when Boy Scout Troop 2 of La Salle was allowed to use a cabin at Camp Ki-Shau-Wau, the area Scout camp. It was important that the cabin be heated, because the weekend we drew was in mid-January. We were ready to go!

We were organized. The first thing we did on arrival was load up on firewood. Having been at the Scout camp during the summer, we knew the firewood was nicely stacked in a shed behind the dining hall, which was closed for the winter. All we had to do was form a firewood brigade and load up the cabin with enough logs for the weekend.

The cabin was big. It would sleep forty quite easily in the double-decker bunk beds. I had selected an upper berth and noticed my brothers also selected upper berths, but never stopped to figure out why we did that.

The firewood brigade returned with a nice supply of logs, and the weather was not too cold, so all we needed was enough heat to take the chill out of the cabin. Off we went to hike around the frozen Scout camp that had seemed so shady and secluded in the summer and now seemed so bleak and crisp. Things we couldn't see without walking long trails during summer days were really just a few feet away in the winter, when there was no foliage to hide the paths.

We built a huge campfire outside our cabin that first night. It was fun cooking our beans and our stew in their cans and our hot dogs and marshmallows on sticks. We ate up heartily. The sun went down.

As the fire dwindled, the cold air began to penetrate our

somewhat wet clothes (wet from hiking to the Vermilion River where we swam in summer and which we tried to walk on, without success, that day). It was time to go in and gather round the potbellied stove in the center of the cabin. It was then that we discovered the wood was gone; we had used it to build that lovely fire outside where we had sung fine Scout songs and heard stories about the escapades of Troop 2 in years past.

The firewood brigade was again called into action. Only the fire brigade informed us they had emptied the wood-shed; we had burned all there was. This, of course, was no problem for Boy Scouts who were taught survival was a time to innovate. We took our flashlights and went into the woods in search of firewood.

Don in BS uniform with Maxwell Freudenberg, Fred Schmoeger, and brother Paul

We returned to the cabin with a fine pile of logs and twigs—enough, we were sure, to last the night. The twigs were wet. So we carefully brought in the smoldering embers of the campfire someone had almost extinguished by dousing it with water and spreading it about. One of the Scouts came from a family that ran a dairy. His contribution to the troop was a case of chocolate milk and a box of straws. We found the straws burned slowly when lit—in fact one could smoke them if one wanted to flirt with lung damage.

We got the small stuff burning only to discover the large stuff was too long to fit in the stove. Out came the Boy Scout hatchets. As blisters formed and wet logs absorbed all the heat from the straws and twigs, the fire ebbed dangerously close to extinction while the now tired Boy Scouts again grabbed their Scout flashlights and headed into the darkness. It was amazing to us how clean the woods were of things that would burn. Maybe leaves would help at least keep the fire going till we found more intermediate-size sticks.

The leaves smoldered, sending billows of smoke throughout the cabin. This required opening doors and windows. We were definitely not getting any warmer. It was now past bedtime for the Scouts, but we labored on till we all had blisters from chopping branches—but not the big ones. They could wait until morning.

We didn't sit around the potbellied stove telling stories and singing songs. We went to bed. Those who had top bunks were up where there was some heat. Oh, yes, now I knew why all three Huling boys had automatically chosen top bunks. We had bunk beds in our unheated bedroom over the garage at home. Any heat entering the room from the house made its way to the upper bunks first.

Before I forget it, we did have a scoutmaster. He had never been a Scout, which became apparent as the weekend progressed. Older boys like my brother Don, an Eagle scout, sort of watched over the scoutmaster.

During the night the weather changed quite drastically. The wind blew, the snow flew, the temperature dropped, and the fire went out. During the night, my brother Don awoke me. He told me to go get one of the cotton mattresses from an empty bunk and sandwich myself under it. He said I would be "like a hot dog in a bun." I did, and it worked.

The next day was a lesson in survival as we chewed all the frozen chocolate milk, ate crackers, cookies, and anything cold. We were not happy campers. As a tenderfoot in rank, I spent the day hunting wood for the night. The snow had not helped.

That night came the real test of Scoutmanship. The smoky potbellied stove caused runny eyes and much coughing, but we finally had a fine fire roaring in the stove. It made large popping noises, then long hissing sounds as it belched forth smoke and heat. We all sandwiched ourselves between mattresses and promptly drifted off, dreaming of home.

No one added fuel to the fire. It went out. The temperature was near zero. The walls were thin. We would have died there except for some man who crept into our cabin during the night. Then he left. When he returned, he had dry wood and coal. He quietly built a fire that didn't smoke. Heat, wonderful heat, began to soothe the dreamers into believing they really were at home in their warm beds.

As the sun rose, there came a hissing noise and the smell of something cooking, something like bacon. Then eggs began to pop and splash grease as they fried. I was awake, wide awake!

And there was my dad, who had come to rescue his three boys and the rest of Troop 2. Man, did we eat! The more we ate, the more the stories we told began to grow in scope and illusions. To hear us tell it, Troop 2 had survived the coldest night on record by rubbing two green sticks together and had built such a roaring fire the doors and windows had to be opened to let the heat out!

But we all knew, deep down, that my dad was an angel that night and early morning. He knew his boys well, and their friends, too, and sensed we needed him on that cold winter campout.

I sure was proud of my dad. Always.

The Reward

OLD MR. NEUSTADT owned and operated a men's clothing store on the corner of Second and Marquette Streets in La Salle. He also owned the entire building that housed many doctor and dentist offices above the store. He was called old Mr. Neustadt because he was timelessly old. He had sold clothing to four generations of some families. Even his son and daughter, who were waiting to take over the business, were old as I first remember them.

Old Mr. Neustadt needed help. He couldn't see well enough to make change, couldn't see the price tags (although he knew prices because he set them), couldn't pull hard enough on the cord to raise the basket containing sold merchandise to the wire which ran from above the counter to the area where the clothes were wrapped and the money received. The money was in a little leather box inside the basket. The basket was powered by a quick pull on a cord. Pull too hard and the basket crashed into the receiving area, frightening the two ladies who worked there. Pull too lightly on the cord and the basket would not reach its destination and slowly, very slowly, drift back to the counter from which it was sent.

So I got the job of being old Mr. Neustadt's helper. I got the job because he tested me on my abilities to add and to make change. The two women who wrapped the clothes and made the change always checked the addition, but old Mr. Neustadt also always checked the addition before sending the basket on its way. Now I was to do his addition and correctly count out the change to the customer. When old Mr. Neustadt tried to count out the change, he often forgot what he was doing, as he was nearly always telling a story to the customer when the basket returned. With me there, he could keep on talking until the story was finished or the customer left.

When there were no customers, I did things like fold shirts and pants, arranging them back in their proper locations by size, or I brushed the men's felt hats to remove dust and slick down the felt, or I sorted men's gloves by pairs and

Neustadt's Clothing Store, 2nd and Marquette, La Salle

sizes or did anything else that needed to be done. I never sat down, as there was no place to sit.

The store opened at 9:00 A.M. and closed at 9:00 P.M., twelve hours later. I had an hour off for lunch and an hour off for dinner, so I walked the six blocks home up Marquette Street and back for each meal.

About 2:00, old Mr. Neustadt needed his two-hour nap. After he left the store, there was a sudden change in the atmosphere. The women who wrapped packages could be heard to giggle, the clerks who manned their stations within the store would drift to a central area and talk in normal tones, and customers would be groaned at before the proper clerk would reluctantly break loose from the pack. Old Mr. Neustadt's son, Bert, and daughter would take over as bosses when he was gone. No clerk paid the slightest bit of attention to Bert, but they would be very polite to the daughter.

Mr. Zevnich, one of the clerks who was friendly to me, told me no one paid attention to the son because he grew up in the store, running around tearing things up till the clerks couldn't stand him anymore. Now the son was old, so Mr. Zevnich had been around a long, long time. The daughter hadn't been allowed in the men's store till she was grown. She made the money change at the basket area, so she was treated with respect. She acted more like the clerks than a boss.

Our friend Darwin, Mr. Zevnich's youngest son

My mother put a stop to my working for old Mr. Neustadt. She said I needed to be spending my Saturdays running off steam in the open air instead of inside a musty old clothing store. She was right. Besides, there were better ways to earn fifty cents, even if I was only eleven years old.

After old Mr. Neustadt died, the store was never the same. The son and daughter sold the building and retired. That was the right thing to do.

I never saw the daughter again, but I saw the son many times. He never recognized me. But Mr. Zevnich got a job in another clothing store and always remembered me with fondness. That was the reward I cherish in my memories.

Route 11—A Good Route to Take

WHEN I WAS eleven years old, I became a partner with an independent businessman named Don. Don was my brother. Our independent business had a name: Route 11. The *Post-Tribune* was the daily newspaper, and it was our very important job to deliver the news quickly to sixty subscribers that made up Route 11.

Don bought and sold 360 newspapers a week (six days a week times sixty papers per day). Collection of money and delivery required about nine hours per week. The pay was $1.80 for the week. We got to keep three cents per paper. Not bad pay for boys ages fourteen and eleven back in 1938. Don loyally paid me fifty cents a week. For that I delivered alone every Friday and helped collect and deliver on Saturdays.

Don was the best in his business and expected me to be just as responsible as he was in all things. He taught me promptness, courtesy, consideration, and honesty. It was fun being his partner.

We were on time. We were the first to turn in our collection money to the *Post-Tribune* each week. Sometimes that meant that Don would take money from his savings. But we owed the *Post-Tribune* at 11:00 A.M. each Saturday, so we were there, sometimes waiting for Miss Josephine Whipple to open the receiving desk.

We delivered papers to the door or to the porch. When the wind might blow the paper away, we would fold, roll, and tuck the papers into a tight roll. In rain and snow, we tried to place all papers behind screen or storm doors.

We accepted delay of payment from customers. Sometimes a customer just didn't have fifteen cents when Saturday came. For others, we had to be clever to get our money. One housewife had a strong compulsion to gamble our fifteen cents before we got there on Saturday mornings. She owed us for three weeks of papers when we decided to collect from her husband on Friday nights. That worked.

Once I cracked a window when I threw the paper. As Don taught me, I knocked on the door of the big house on the northeast corner of Seventh and Joliet Streets, confessed, and offered to pay to repair the damage. Instead of being angry, Mr. Duncan praised my integrity and gave me a tip. We never threw Mr. Duncan's paper again; we carried it all the way up the long walk, across the porch, and placed a nonrolled paper behind his storm door.

Our bundle of sixty papers was dropped off promptly at 3:30 P.M. at a point about five blocks from our home on Marquette Street. Regardless of all events and weather, Don taught me to be there when they arrived. Our customers expected their papers on time—4:30 at the latest—or we received phone calls asking what happened. One customer, Sadie, the last one on our route, would call about 4:15. We finally went out of our way to make her one of our first customers. As a reward, she paid us in Indian-head pennies. We traded them to a neighbor boy, Max Freudenburg, at face value.

One time the *Post-Tribune* asked us to turn in a list of names and addresses of all our customers. All went well until we tried to communicate with an elderly man who was deaf and only spoke Polish. We finally gave him a name we made up—Deafguyski. About a year later his son visited and told me his name was Debrowski or something close to that. Don and I figured we were so close we'd leave it as Deafguyski. Nobody noticed.

When Don retired from Route 11, the *Post-Tribune* granted me ownership. What Don had taught me about work habits stayed with me. They are still with me. Don should be proud to know that. I know I am of him.

The Watermelon

IT WAS A hot, muggy summer day about 1939 when my brother Don and I spotted an overloaded, stake-bodied truck piled high with watermelons pulling up to a stop in front of the Urbanowski Grocery Store, where we were taking a break from delivering newspapers. Watermelons were a luxury during the Depression, so we didn't eat much watermelon at our house. Don had never even acquired a taste for them, and I didn't care one way or the other for them, as they seemed bothersome to eat.

But my Grandmother Hawthorne from Kansas thought watermelon was great! Where she lived, there was an abundance of melons. And she was visiting our home in La Salle the day this overloaded truck arrived. The truck was very old, obviously a farm truck, and the man who drove it looked like a poor person. Maybe we could afford a watermelon for Grandmother?

Don and I sat in the shade of the store awning, drinking ice-cold bottles of pop, as the man entered the store. Soon he returned and began unloading melons. He had a smile on his face. Apparently he had made a large sale (and it sure looked like he could use the money).

The problem was, he could only unload one melon at a time! Working by himself, the poor man had to climb from street level up the side of the truck, all the way to the top, reach out for a melon from the top of the pile, then jump to the ground, turning in the air, holding the melon. We offered to help before the man overworked himself and collapsed from the heat. He couldn't believe it! He acted as if we had been sent from heaven. He was already hot from driving his truck who knows how far, and here he was, leaping, climbing, and trying not to drop those melons. He really needed help!

Don and I were young teenagers, not full-grown, but every day we carried Don's heavy newspapers in a canvas shoulder bag, so we were in pretty good shape. First Don offered the man the use of his newspaper bag. The man would fill it with two melons, then lower it to one of us to unload on the sidewalk. This helped, but it was still too slow.

Finally the man asked, "Can you catch?" He tossed a melon to Don, who staggered under the load, but caught it. Then he tried me. Golly, they were big and heavy, but I didn't want to be outdone by my big brother, so I learned to catch melons quite gracefully that day. I felt really grown-up!

When we finished unloading about a hundred melons, we were soaked with sweat, and our pop, what was left of it, was warm. The man rewarded us by giving each of us a melon.

That evening Don and I found out that watermelon was delicious. Maybe it was because we had worked so hard to earn the two melons! Our grandmother thought we had done it all for her. And maybe we had.

❋   ❋   ❋

Dog Day

IT WAS A warm late summer day while I was riding my bicycle loaded with my afternoon newspapers to be delivered, when out of nowhere a large gray-and-dirty-white dog attacked me. It scared me because he was snarling and snapping at my legs. I had been approached by dogs before while riding my bike, but could normally talk to the dog or, if necessary, shout to get down. Sometimes I would even stop and

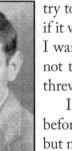

James Urbanski

try to make friends with a dog, especially if it was one who lived on my paper route. I wanted a dog to be glad to see me and not think that the newspapers I held, or threw, were a threat.

I had seen the dog that attacked me before. It didn't really belong to anyone, but my friend Jim, from two blocks away, had tried to make friends with it over a period of days. He wasn't having much luck. The dog was not happy. Most of the kids left the dog alone, or avoided it altogether.

But it got me! It grabbed my pant cuff and caused me, my bike, and my full load of newspapers to crash in the yard of my very first customer, who was standing behind her screen door waiting for me to hand her a paper.

Mrs. Donovan, the customer, stood helplessly as the dog commenced to jump at me and bite me over and over again. I screamed for help, but none came. I shouted at the dog to get down, sit, stay—anything! But the dog would not obey.

Newspapers were spread across the yard and were all I could reach, so I grabbed a rolled-up newspaper and swung it at the dog. The dog backed off after I hit it a few times, then very angrily turned tail, snarling at me as it reluctantly withdrew with its tail between its legs. It threatened to return, but I shouted in my meanest voice and shook the newspaper. It slunk off toward Jim's house.

Mrs. Donovan, an elderly woman, told me to go home quickly before the dog attacked me again, that she would watch my newspapers and try to pick them up if the dog was not around.

Lucky for me, my dad was home when I entered the house crying in pain. One look at me and he ordered me into the bathtub, where he could wash and examine my bloody wounds. I remember the pain from the bites, but I don't recall the pain of Dad swabbing my wounds with alcohol, witch hazel, and Mercurochrome, each one following the other, before he bandaged me.

As I dressed, Dad phoned the police and told them to meet him at Donovans' house in five minutes. He was angry! He carried a hammer as we went.

I delivered my papers, Dad talked to the police, and Mrs. Donovan told them where she thought the dog was at the time. Mrs. Donovan had carefully reassembled almost all my newspapers, but I had to call in for some replacements that were too torn up to deliver.

Many customers asked me why I was so late delivering my papers that day, but quickly forgave me when they saw how bad I looked. I seemed to hurt everywhere.

My friend, Jim Urbanski, came to my house later on and told me the dog wasn't his and he had not known what to do with it. Jim and I became better friends that day.

The police shot the dog on the spot where they located it. I never went to a doctor. I guess the dog wasn't rabid.

PART III

HIGH SCHOOL ADVENTURES

Growing-up Years

MANY OF MY friends were the oldest boys in their families and got new clothes from time to time. I remember admiring their new things and being glad when brother Don outgrew his black suit and gave it to brother John. There was only eighteen months difference between Don and John, and between John and me. Don gave up the suit at the end of winter, and John grew so much all summer that I got the suit that fall. I was pretty impressed with that! Here I was wearing a suit when my friends were considered to be too young for one. They still wore knickers and Buster Browns (which I never owned), while I was in a suit with long pants!

One year there was no hand-me-down winter jacket for me, so I wore my dad's old college sweater. I thought I would start a new fad, but Mom didn't care for that look and I got a coat instead. About six years later, every girl in high school wore baggy sweaters all winter and wouldn't be caught dead in a coat. But boys still wore coats.

There were things I wanted to do but my folks couldn't afford, or maybe it was things they wanted me to do but couldn't afford, so I helped. At least two of these things were great for me: my flute lessons, for which I paid half, and ballroom dancing lessons, for which I paid all. These expenses were met by my helping brother Don with his paper route until he was old enough to get a better job, and then he gave the route to me. That route paid for a lot, as Don took violin and dancing lessons and took Lindy, his girlfriend, on dates. And I've enjoyed music and dancing all my life.

As a kid I had no two-wheeled bicycle, other than the one I bought for ten cents once. Later I bought a bike for five dollars that I rode twenty miles a day on paper routes and to places in general for many years. I sold it during the war for fifteen dollars—a bargain.

About 1939, when I didn't have five dollars, a bunch of us boys were playing baseball behind the Congregational Church on the northeast corner of Fifth and Joliet Streets when an old man who lived nearby came and asked us if we wanted to buy his car. It was a beautiful green-and-black Model T, which he kept in a garage. It ran quite well, and, of course, we would have loved to have it even though we were only twelve or thirteen years old. The old man was so in need of money he had to sell the car. We had to tell him no, and now I wonder if we told anyone in our neighborhood or the church how desperate the old man was.

The first time I ever heard a radio was when we went to Baird's Grocery Store with Mom one day. There sat Mr. Baird in front of a box with a large oval horn-shaped thing on top of it, which made squealy and static noises as he turned the dial. We had to wait as Mr. Baird adjusted the radio; then, when he had some nice music—with static—he waited on Mom. He wanted the best for his store. Later he took the radio into the back room because it was a distraction to shoppers, or because customers thought he was rich and could add more debts to their account. I'm not sure which.

Almost every day someone from my family would go to Baird's for groceries because we didn't own a refrigerator. We had an icebox and the cold garage. In the summer a sign in the window would tell the Callahan brothers how many pounds of ice to deliver. In the winter we used the garage to store food or make ice to use in the icebox. But for ice cream we generally went to Little Billie's, a couple blocks away. He hand-packed Orsingers ice cream and made sure there were

LaSalle Theatre

no air spaces as he packed. Sometimes we hand-cranked our own ice-cream maker, but that was a lot of work and cost us a lot of ice from the icebox. It sure was good, though.

We didn't spend much money—we didn't have it. The first movie I remember cost five cents at the Roxy Theater. It was about a World War I flying ace, Bulldog Drummond, I think. It had sound and lots of fancy flying. Movies went up to a dime when the Roxy closed, then up to fifteen cents for better movies in a better theater. Adults paid a quarter at the La Salle Theater on First Street and the Majestic on Gooding between First and Second Streets.

Until La Salle got a swimming pool, we swam in Peru for a nickel. One day I rode my fenderless bike to Peru over Shooting Park Road, which was gravel and quite rough and dusty. Going home it was not dusty. It had been oiled. By the time I got home, I had a black streak up the front and down the back.

Majestic Theatre

We took the bus to travel from La Salle to Peru at night. Cost: five cents. Sometimes we rode the bus around the entire route a couple times just to see who got on and off. One rainy night when I got caught in a rain after work on a Saturday night, all I had was a five-dollar bill. This had to have been about 1944 for me to have had that much money. The cranky old bus driver got mad at me and began counting out nickels for change for the five-dollar bill. By the time he got to about three dollars in nickels, I told him I wanted off at the next stop. Then he really went into a rage at me! About then, a very large man from the back of the bus stepped up and took hold of the collar of the bus driver and told him to take back those nickels and give me dollar bills. He said a few more things to the driver that put fear in the driver's heart. I never had trouble with that driver again, but then I never hoped to try his patience again, either.

Many, many of my classmates quit school to work full-time when they turned sixteen. By then the war was on and jobs were plentiful. The twenty-dollars-a-week jobs looked too good to pass up. Then, some war jobs started paying double that, and we lost more kids to work. They never had it so good, and it was soon parted from most of them. By eighteen, most of us boys were in the services, and when we got out an education was more important, unless you accepted a twenty-five-dollars-a-week dead-end labor job.

Musical Memories

CHURCH WAS VERY important to us as kids. As families, we went to church night potluck suppers. After supper we kids played hide-and-seek using the entire darkened church. We wanted to go to Sunday school to see our friends. We sang in the children's choir because we wanted to contribute our talent of music. We played our instruments in a Sunday school orchestra because it was fun and gave us a chance to play something besides what a music teacher would assign. The orchestra had a wide range of instruments, ages, and talent. That didn't make any difference; the older kids encouraged the younger ones to play. Brother Don played violin, John the cello, Max Freudenberg clarinet, Tom Seaton trumpet, Dawn Harris violin, and Portia Harris viola. I played my flute. Once for about a year, we didn't have an adult leader, but we continued on until we got one. If my memory is correct, the girl on piano, Lindy, my brother Don's future wife, retired and turned the job over to Jean, my future wife. "Follow the Gleam" was our closing number for the kids to sing as they marched off to class.

What I remember most about Sunday school was a boys' class that met in the church kitchen about 1938. There was a very large cast-iron gas stove into which we put one of the

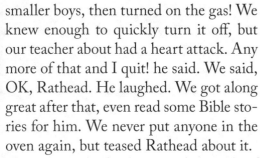
Musical Family

Jean Hahne

Lindy Marshall

smaller boys, then turned on the gas! We knew enough to quickly turn it off, but our teacher about had a heart attack. Any more of that and I quit! he said. We said, OK, Rathead. He laughed. We got along great after that, even read some Bible stories for him. We never put anyone in the oven again, but teased Rathead about it.

During the late 1930s, the youth of the church formed a group called the Youth Fellowship that met on Sunday nights. We mostly socialized, but read some religious material, too. We were organized for business meetings with a president, vice president, secretary, and treasurer. We paid a nickel a week to the treasurer. When the treasury had over five dollars, we usually gave it to a worthy cause around the church.

About 1939, someone gave the church a sound system for the hearing impaired. It might have been Ralph Lefler or Harry Swegar. There were earphones in some of the pews and speakers in the social hall and a turntable for playing recorded music!

It didn't take us long to make use of the turntable. It started out with a few old records donated by church members, but some teenagers brought their latest 78 rpm hit parade records from home so we could listen and dance as our entertainment after the meeting. Soon we used our treasury money to purchase up-to-date records rather than give the money away. That raised some eyebrows. Then we voted to hold a dance after a football game and charge ten cents to get in. We sold pop for a nickel. We paid the church custodian to set up and clean up. (We would have done it, but he needed the work and extra money.) The dances became a sensation! For years they helped keep the youth of the church active and provided a place for town kids to go to dance. We voted to give the Ladies Aid Society fifteen dollars. That helped keep us in business, but almost wiped us out for new records.

Was This the Right Thing to Do?!

BACK ABOUT THE year 1940, I found $41.55 on the floor of the local teenage hangout, The Igloo. (It really wasn't $41.55, it was $5.00. But in today's dollars, that $5.00 was worth $41.55.) When I was fourteen years old, $5.00 was worth ten weeks' allowance money, two weeks of paperboy money, and more money than I had in my bank account. In awe of the bill, I picked it up.

Pat Mazzorana

Louie Mazzorana

With the $5.00 tucked safely into my pocket and no one noticing that I had picked it up, I sat quietly at the soda bar and observed the people around me. First, I wanted to be sure no one saw me retrieve it, and secondly, I wondered which of the many people could have dropped it and not missed it! I checked my pocket every minute or so to make sure I still had that $5.00; I expected anyone else who had that kind of money to check their pockets just as often.

But fate was present. I soon spotted a woman searching her purse. The more she searched, the more anxiety she showed. She became frantic. She searched the floor, she looked at people like she was about to ask them something. As she peered into one face and then another, I turned away so she wouldn't catch me looking. I became uneasy.

She approached Louie, the highly respected owner of The Igloo. With tears flowing freely, she spilled out her dilemma, which I could overhear. This $5.00 had been her grocery money for her family. It was her only allowance for the coming week. Her family would suffer. Couldn't Louie help?

Louie assured her that he would tell her if the money showed up. She faded into the crowd.

I couldn't stand it. I gave Louie the $5.00.

Louie looked at me long and hard. He studied me. He wanted to say something, I could tell, but all he said was, "Thanks, Boah." Boah was Louie's expression for everyone he didn't know by name. With hundreds of kids frequenting The Igloo, you were special if Louie knew your name. When said in a certain way, Boah sounded like boy, Bill, Bob, or even Paul if you used your imagination. My brothers, Don and John, both thought it sounded like Don and John; that's how cleverly Louie could say Boah.

The woman cried with joy when Louie handed her the $5.00. Although I really wanted to remain anonymous, I had not told Louie to keep it quiet. I was therefore subjected to hugs and praises from this woman, whom I didn't know.

I felt good about the praises, good about the looks Louie gave me, and about the first reactions of the people and friends around me. Then I felt embarrassed about the hugs. And finally, I began to feel rather badly. No reward? Not even a milk shake or a Coke? Some friends commented that I should have kept my mouth shut. I had the urge to leave. I thought about all the things I could have done with that $5.00. Just a few weeks before this, I could have bought a nice Model T Ford that ran real well and looked sharp for $5.00. Of course, I was too young and didn't have that much.

Then came the blow. The woman asked Louie for change—four one-dollar bills and change. She used the change to play the slot machine. (Slot machines were legal in this town.) She was a new person. Her fortune had been lost, but now it was found! She would celebrate, I thought. And she did. She asked Louie for change—a dollar

Pat and Louie

at a time—until it was all gone! She felt great! Her family would starve, and she felt great? I was angry, I was puzzled, I was in pain inside.

I dug into my pocket to see if I had the five cents to take the bus home. I went home alone, left my friends behind. I usually waited until the last bus and ran for it at the last second, like the rest of my friends. That night I left early. I wondered if I had done the right thing.

I have long since concluded that I couldn't have kept that money, because other events have occurred that tell me so. Yet, to this day, I wonder if I contributed to that woman's problem.

But one thing of which I am very proud is that the next time I went to The Igloo, Louie said to me, all 115 pounds of me standing six feet tall, "Hey, Boah, why do they call you Fat?"

A Clever Chief

ONE SATURDAY NIGHT, the gang of kids that hung around together somehow gathered at Betty Lou's house when her parents were not home. What probably happened was that Betty Lou had to house-sit her younger brothers and had phoned the Igloo to suggest to her friend, Paula, that she was lonely and wanted company.

Betty Lou's house was just across the street from where the local buses would stop for passengers, so about ten of us left the Igloo and went to Betty Lou's.

What we normally did on evenings like this was sit around and listen to each other, the radio, or records, and drink Cokes—which Betty Lou's parents seemed to have in unlimited supply and did not mind when we young visitors helped ourselves.

It was autumn, warm and dry outside. Inside, in the basement, a load of coal had been delivered that contained hundreds of crickets! Betty Lou's little brothers were down there catching them, to throw them outside, so I went down to help them.

The upstairs group decided to go outside and enjoy the nice weather. One boy, Jim, tossed a Coke bottle to another boy and hollered, "Geronimo!"

The boy caught it, dropped back, and threw it back, yelling "Geronimo!"

Jim caught it, then dropped way back into the darkness beyond the light radiating from the single bulb of the street light above the bus stop, and threw a long one. He yelled, but no one saw it.

Remember now, this is what I was told because I wasn't there, I was in the basement—where it suddenly turned pitch black as the electrical power failed. The small boys had to lead me out of the basement as I tried to keep them calm.

What had happened was the Coke bottle hit the electric pole and broke a wire that powered the entire neighborhood, including the street light.

The party was over. We all went home, but not before Jim had instructed us all as to what we would say if anyone asked us what we knew about it. The story was to be that some out of town guys were driving around the neighborhood and got into an argument with us, and as they drove off they threw the pop bottle.

Next day, Sunday, after lunch the phone rang and my dad answered. After talking a couple of minutes he handed me the phone and said, "It's Chief Mike Kasprowitz, he wants to ask you some questions." As I took the phone he said simply, "Just tell him the truth."

Thurman Huling

Dad didn't accent *truth,* like I had something to hide. He didn't accent *tell* like I would hold something back. And he didn't accent *him* like the Chief of Police was someone special or that he was intimidating. He just plain said, "Just tell him the truth" like he expected me to do exactly that, the way I would tell the truth to him if he asked me anything, about anything.

The Chief asked me what happened at Betty Lou's house last night.

I told him about the crickets and the blackout.

Then he asked, "Who threw the bottle?"

"I think it was Jim," I said.

"Let me talk to your dad again," he said.

When Dad hung up he said, "The Chief keeps a close watch over you and your friends. He was worried that some kids from outside of town might have been around making trouble, but you cleared it up."

Next day, in school, Betty Lou told us the power company had the lights back on within an hour. The power company told her dad they had fixed it so it wouldn't happen again. The police had arrived at the scene, making a list of names from Betty Lou. She thought someone had already called and told them about a "wild party" going on. That was all Betty Lou knew about it.

Jim had been called by the Chief first. I wondered why until I thought about who on the names given to him would be the most likely to get into trouble. I must have been the next one called.

Jim began bragging that his made-up story had worked. I told him it hadn't, that all the police cared about was that outsiders weren't causing trouble in our town.

Jim thought a minute, then said, "H'm. Then why did the

Chief call me back and tell me to be sure and call the police if I ever see those outsiders doing weird stuff again?"

"Think about it," I said to Jim. "The Chief didn't care about the light, but you'd better tell him the straight story next time you do something stupid, because he'll find out one way or the other."

My opinion of the Chief went up a notch.

Tobacco and Me
by Don Huling

THE LAST NATIONAL Cornhusking Contest was held near Tonica, Illinois, the fall of 1940. It was a big event, and people came from all over the U.S.A. to see the cornhuskers compete. I had spent enough time on my Huling grandparents' farm to know how these men worked. The ear of corn was broken off the stalk, and the husk was removed by using a glove with a hook on it. The hook laid the husk open so the ear of corn could be yanked out and thrown into a wagon. The contestants were penalized if they threw fodder into the wagon. They were also penalized if they missed an ear of corn and left it in the field. It was a sight to behold when the starting gun was fired and about a dozen men started throwing ears of corn against the buckboard as they walked down their corn row. The wagon was pulled with a tractor, and a judge rode in the wagon. If the ear of corn missed the buckboard, that was also a penalty.

The whole place had a carnival atmosphere. Tents on both sides of the midway were selling stuff and even giving it away. That's when John Wacker and I made our big mistake.

They were passing out Redman Chewing Tobacco in small paper containers—one to every customer who visited

their tent. John and I each got a bag and decided immediately to give it a try. We had seen how baseball players
always had a big chaw in their mouths from movies of
Dizzy Dean, our favorite ballplayer. My grandfather Huling liked a chew now and then, too. My grandmother made
him chew outside, as it was a dirty habit, especially if you
missed the cuspidor. Anyway, we tore open the package
and stuffed the entire wad into our mouths all at once. The
wad made our cheeks stick out—just like Dizzy Dean's.

Right away something started to go wrong. We both felt
awful sick and dizzy. In fact we got so lightheaded we had to
lie down right in the field where they were parking cars.

Somehow we got home and lived to tell our tale. Tobacco
and I were not meant to get along. Later I tried cigarettes but
didn't do any better. The heck with it, I decided. I don't have
to be like the other guys. Rather than see my money go up in
smoke, I'll save it. And I did.

The Old Model A
by Don Huling

DAD WAS WITH me the first time I drove her. We
were up north of town on a gravel road, so I drove the
Model A home and even put her in the garage. Boy, was that
fun! Dad and I agreed that I should get my driver's license
as soon as I could. The next Saturday we went down and applied at Terry Martin's. In about two weeks the notice came
for me to go to Ottawa to take my driver's test. I took off
from school, and Mother and I made the trip. I drove all the
way and came through the test with flying colors. From then
on, the hardest question—but one most frequently asked of
Dad—was, "Can I have the car, Pop?"

Dad bought the car way back in 1929 and was really in style for those days. He had a trunk put on it, as he knew there had to be someplace to put the luggage when we all headed to Ohio. My earliest recollections of trips taken in Betsy, as we came to call her, were trips back east to visit Dad's parents on the farm. It became a yearly affair.

I remember how we would pack the night before and get up about four in the morning to get an early start. We would leave La Salle just as the sky began to turn yellow. Paul, being the smallest, usually sat in the front seat with Mom and Dad, while Alice, John, and I got to take up the whole backseat. As the years passed, Paul got tired of sitting in front where it was crowded. John and I would trade places with him now and then. Invariably when John and Paul got in back together, a quarrel or fight ensued.

It was an all-day trip at forty miles per hour. We all became especially restless as we neared the farm. There was a big hill just before we got there, and I remember how it seemed we would never get up the other side fast enough.

The first (and perhaps the last!) Model A Ford in La Salle.

The day I first took my girl, Lindy, for a ride was the beginning of a new era. I bet Betsy could have found her way

Glenn, Lindy, Nip or Tuck

out to 112 Gunn Avenue by herself after a couple of years. I was a junior, and Lindy was a sophomore.

I didn't get the car much for dates at first, but the summer I returned from the farm and started school as a senior, things were different. Lindy and I had been going steady for almost a year, so on Friday night, which was date night, I usually got the car to take my gal to the football game and The Igloo. Lindy would invite me in, and if her folks had gone to bed, I'd stay awhile.

If they hadn't, I'd come in anyway, and after a few hints, Lindy's mom would finally get up and follow Glenn up to bed. Guess she knew what was on our minds.

I'd get Betsy home sometime after midnight, sometimes coasting into the garage so as not to make too much noise. I'd lock the back door and head for the bathroom, where I'd undress and get ready for bed. Mom would be awake, but nothing much was said. I was always in too big a hurry to get to my upper bunk on the sleeping porch. I'd go to sleep dreaming about my beautiful girlfriend.

After football season came the basketball games. The weather really turned cold. This didn't stop us from our Friday night dates and visits to The Igloo. The car didn't have a heater, so Lindy would take the blanket we always carried in winter and curl up next to me. I'd make a beeline for Peru over Shooting Park Road, which was still gravel in those days.

Gee, it felt good to get to Louie's and smell the porks and French fries cooking out in the kitchen. When it wasn't too crowded we would get our table over by the register, but usually we had to grab the first one we came across. We would put in our order for a pork tenderloin and fries, then listen to the jukebox play Glenn Miller songs. "String of Pearls" was my favorite. To this day, every time I hear that song, it brings back memories of The Igloo.

After a cup of hot coffee, it was another rush out to the cold, cold car and home again by way of Shooting Park Road. The Marshall home had a hot-air register Lindy would stand near as soon as we got to her place. They also had a nice couch we occupied for a while before I had to leave for that cold sleeping porch.

Spring arrived at last, and so did my high-school graduation. A group of us kids had a midnight picnic out at Starved Rock. Lindy and I watched the sun rise that morning; then we drove home to Lindy's place. I was so sleepy I fell asleep on the couch. Lindy's dad got a big laugh out of that, but my Grandmother Hawthorne didn't think it was a laughing matter when she found out I hadn't come home that night. She was staying with us boys while Mom and Dad took the train out to Oberlin, Ohio, to see Alice graduate from college. All was forgiven, and life continued for two teenagers very much in love.

I spent that summer of 1941 working on my Huling grandparents' farm in Ohio. Man, it really was good getting back home again to La Salle. I dressed up and headed old Betsy up north. Boy, did I ever get a warm welcome from Lindy. I had called as soon as I got home and made a date.

As I drove up, there was Lindy standing on the sidewalk in one of her summer dresses, waiting to greet me. I'd been looking forward to that moment for so long. It was swell to get back home.

December 7, 1941, the day the Japanese bombed Pearl Harbor, was a turning point for the whole world. I continued to go to school at LPO Junior College and date my sweetheart.

We were apart again the summer of 1942 when I attended Rolla School of Mines and lived with my uncle Fred Hawthorne, who was a civil engineer working for the U.S. government. Fort Leonard Wood, southwest of Rolla, Missouri, was being rapidly expanded to handle the flood of young men my age entering the U.S. Army.

When I returned home I got a job, saved some money, and rode my bicycle over to Cohard Jewelry Store, where I bought a diamond engagement ring. I showed the ring to my mother, whose remark was, "Don, you know when you give this to Lindy, it is serious business!"

Don, 1944, France

Pretty Lindy

"I know, Mom," I replied. "I want to marry her as soon as I can." Little did I realize that in a little more than a year, we would be man and wife.

The old Model A passed from hand to hand, and if she could have talked she would have been able to tell many more tales. She got us to where we wanted to go—and after all, what more is expected from a car?!

Don't Race Cars
by Don Huling

W E GOT STOPPED by the Spring Valley police, and I wound up paying the fine. Here is how I remember getting into this fix.

Frank Hess and I were L-P High School buddies. We both played in the high-school orchestra and were in the same class of '41. Lindy and I had double-dated with Betty and "Fritz" along with Jack Hess and his date. We at-

Frank "Fritz" Hess

tended a movie at the Majestic Theater entitled *The Cat and the Canary,* starring Paulette Goddard. The only seats we could find for six of us together were up in the last row of the balcony. The movie was a scary one, and I was sitting on the edge of my seat. Right at the spooky part, Jack reached over and pinched me. I let out a yell heard all over the theater and jumped right out of the seat. Those Hess boys liked to have a good time!

On another Saturday night, for some reason neither Fritz nor

Dick Sharpe

Dick Faletti

I had our dates with us. That's probably why we got into the jam I started to tell about. Fritz had his brother's '41 Ford and had picked my brother John and me up to go "slumming." We decided to go out to Hicks Park at the west end of Spring Valley and listen to a swing band playing there.

We ran into Dick Sharpe and Dick Faletti, probably at one of the hot spots in La Salle, which was wide open back then. They were driving a brand-new Buick—probably Dick Sharp's dad's car. Mr. Sharpe was president of the La Salle National Bank.

We all decided to head for Spring Valley, driving both cars.

Once we got through Peru and past The Igloo, the race was on. We had the older car, but it would really go, and we tore down Route 6 with the two older Dicks in the lead. As we headed down the hill into Spring Valley, we saw their car in the right lane with its taillights on. "Let's take them," we all shouted to Fritz, who was doing a swell job of keeping up with the two veterans ahead of us. We swung into the left lane and zoomed around them—and around the Spring Valley police car. Fritz double-clutched and threw the car into second as we came to a fast stop. He was too smart to try to outrun the cops. I was the only one with enough money on me to pay the fine.

When we caught up to the older guys out at Hicks Park, they had the laugh on us. Seems they had had a similar run-in with police a few weeks earlier, but had gotten wise and remembered the cop's unmarked car's license number.

Moral of story: Don't race!

The second race I got into was with Ralph Schmoeger. For some reason I always got into races when Lindy was not in the car. This time she was at home with her mom and heard the crash when my dad's Model A hit the curb, spun around, and landed on its side.

Ralph and I were heading home to La Salle after visiting some of our high-school friends out at The Igloo in Peru. Back

"Hot Spots" where we went "slumming"

Kelly and Cawley
First Street, LaSalle
Maples
Shooting Park Road, Peru
Stables
St. Vincent Avenue, LaSalle
Del Rio Club
3rd Floor, Water Street, Peru
City Limits Inn
N. St. Vincent, LaSalle
Silver Congo
First and Gooding, LaSalle
Hawaiian Room
Peru Hotel
El Mirador
Hotel Francis, Peru
South Bluff
Peru
Rose Bowl
Vendom Hotel
Diamond Horseshoe
Oglesby
Auditorium
First and Wright, LaSalle
Hicks Park
Spring Valley

in those days, Shooting Park Road was still only gravel at the west end of Peru. Once we both got onto the blacktop road, the race was on. Ralph, who was driving a newer car, was in the lead all the way to La Salle. When he slowed down at the hill just before going up to Creve Coeur Street, I gunned the old Model A and passed him going down the hill. But that is when I got into trouble. There was a sharp turn at the top of the next hill, and I was in the wrong lane going way too fast to navigate it. I pulled the steering wheel to the right at what I thought was the right moment, but the rear left wheel hit the curb. This spun the car around, and it landed on the driver's side.

The Marshalls lived only two blocks up the street. Lindy heard the crash and wondered who was making so much noise.

Ralph pulled up in back of the overturned Ford as I climbed out of the passenger's side window. Luckily no one was hurt, and the car didn't even have a dent in it. Ralph and I pushed the car back on its wheels, and I was able to drive it home. I told my mom and dad, who were in bed by this late hour, what had happened. They were happy that no one was hurt.

The only things that got hurt were my ego and the car tires. The sidewalls of all four tires were weakened from the spin and crash. We had to replace all four tires on our way back to the farm in Ohio. I should have paid for them, but Dad let me off the hook.

Racing automobiles is not a smart thing to do!

My First Plane Ride

WHEN AN AIRPLANE flew over my small home-town, heads would rise and eyes would search the skies for a glimpse of the flying machine. Kids would cry out, "There goes Lindbergh," or "That's the China Clipper" if the plane had more than one engine. Well, you can imagine the excitement one sunny Sunday afternoon when a bi-winger flew over our town, did a loop-de-loop, stalled, dove, and buzzed the very street where I lived!

"Wow! He must be a barnstormer and will give us a ride if we just follow him out of town and find his landing field," we rejoiced.

So we did it! I don't know how I became so lucky that day, but I was with my brother's fiancée, Lindy, and a friend of ours called Gabby. Gabby had received a beautiful blue '31 Chevy convertible for a high-school graduation present. It had one major flaw, however, and that was the tires. With no other tires available during the war, Gabby stayed in town with his car, and even then had to be very careful lest a boot fly out or a patch give way, because it was walk home if a tire went, and there was no spare that would hold air. But he was working on that.

Gabby had just enlisted in the U.S. Army Air Force, in which my brother was already serving. Gabby wanted to be a pilot, so he offered to take the three of us out of town in search of the landing strip. He drove very carefully over U.S. Route 6 east of town. The road was in terrible shape because highway maintenance was nonexistent at that time, and Route 6 had some chunks missing.

We found the airstrip at the Four Corners, as the intersection was known. Gabby literally ran to the plane to procure our tickets. This ride was going to cost me a week's wages, but I was caught up in Gabby's enthusiasm and had always wondered how it would feel to fly in a plane.

We didn't have to wait long. The plane came wobbling toward us, just like in the movies. It made crackling noises from the engine and backfired blue-orange shots that sent puffs of dark blue-black smoke around the plane. When it hit the ground, on one wheel first, it shook so badly, rattling all sorts of loose-joint noises, and bounced so high it almost didn't come down again. I was sure it would flip over, crash on its nose, or just spin out. But the agile pilot had complete control, according to Gabby, and was just showing off for the crowd.

The pilot, with his oily helmet, goggles, and old flying jacket, whizzed up to the crowd and at the last instant spun the plane around, shutting off the noisy engine as the people fanned out in a half run, not knowing what the fool thing was going to do next. It let out one last backfire, which drifted through the audience leaving a very oily smell in the air.

The plane had two seats—one for the pilot and the front one for passengers. So the three of us crammed into the one seat. As we buckled up, the pilot was pouring oil into the engine and wiping off the windshields, which were so covered with oil we couldn't see out. But that was OK; we'd be looking out over the sides like a World War I flying ace would do, wouldn't we?

As I sat waiting, I looked over the crowd which stood in awe, then at the plane, which was really something amazing when examined closely. It was some kind of plane made after World War I, but not much after. The two wings were covered with cloth patches, some of which were quite loose at the edges and flapped in the breeze. Wires crisscrossed from the upper wing to the lower wing. Most of the wires were loose and sagged, as did the wings. The bright paint job was awful up close, but it looked quite sleek from half a mile distance.

I never heard such a syncopated racket in all my life as when that engine started up. It coughed, it wheezed, it shot blue flames, yellow flames, missed beats till it almost came to rest, then coughed and belched some more, revving—only to go through the routine again. Then suddenly, as I was watching the wings shake and rattle, the engine roared to a screaming pitch and the plane lurched forward, oil spraying our clean windshield and our hair, and bounced us uncontrollably through the field of clover hay.

The three of us were all screaming at once about what the others should know, or see, but the noise from the engine drove all other sounds to the wind.

Then we lifted off the ground. For a while everything became quite serene and smooth, or was it that our ears were pressurizing and we couldn't hear? Then the wings began to "take hold"—that is, adjust themselves to the weight of the plane. The wires that crisscrossed from wing to wing began to tune up; they would go from slack to taut then back to slack. Of course, my stomach was telling me it wasn't the wings that were flapping, it was me going up and down at a sickening frequency.

Lindy was in the middle and couldn't see anything. Neither Gabby nor I could see anything either, because every time we put our heads over the edge of the cockpit we were drenched with oil spraying from the engine. No wonder the pilot wore goggles and a helmet!

But the pilot was very considerate. As soon as we got high enough, he tilted the plane about 90 degrees so we could all look down—and squash whoever was on the bottom. This maneuver caused the plane to drop, so to regain speed, the pilot would change from 90 degrees back to a nosedive. Then we would climb again, so steeply we were no longer moving forward but hanging, in a stall. Planes don't like stalls; they fall from the sky. But that was OK; the pilot would somehow get the thing facing downward again. Of course, my stomach was still way up there till we hit bottom and pulled out, then my stomach was way down there!

When we landed, I was very proud of myself; I had not gotten sick! However, I could hardly walk and thought how embarrassing it was going to be when I barfed in front of my friends and all those people. I held it down, feeling worse for doing so. Meanwhile, the pilot was checking the wires and adding more oil to the engine.

On the way home Gabby raved over the experience, but I was pretty quiet. I was thinking, Never again. Flying is not for me. But funny thing, we didn't seem the least concerned about whether Gabby's tires would make it back to town! We were more concerned that the next people who paid money to ride in that thing would be as lucky as we were and survive.

Jobs I Had While Growing Up
by Don Huling

MONEY WAS SCARCE when I was growing up in the late '20s and early '30s. Some of the first money I made as a kid was for shoveling snow. Fifty cents for shoveling the sidewalk out to the street and the sidewalk in front of the house was pretty good pay back in those days.

I got a paper route when I entered high school. I had sixty-six customers that I had to collect fifteen cents from each week. I usually spent Saturday morning collecting this money so I could be one of the first newsboys to get downtown to the newspaper office and pay them twelve cents for each paper they sold me. Most of my customers would meet me at the door with their fifteen cents, but I had one or two who would hold out until Monday or even Tuesday. They were a pain in the you-know-what, but they did teach me perseverance.

The summer of my senior year in high school I spent on my grandfather Huling's farm in Ohio. He and Wilbur Hart needed help harvesting the wheat. Grandpa drove the binder with a team of horses. This machine would cut the wheat and bind it into bales with twine. Grandpa would pull a lever when four or five bales had been accumulated. This action would throw the bales onto the field into rows. My job was to gather up seven or eight bales, stack them head up into shocks, then take another bale and spread it out on top of the shock to sort of act as a lid in case it rained before thrashing time. I worked without a shirt on until Grandma got concerned I'd get too much sun. I sure got thirsty doing that job, and I remember how good and refreshing the well water tasted and felt when I got in from the field.

George Bailey operated the steam-driven thrashing machine. That summer of 1941, I was water boy. Ten or twelve farmers got together and helped each other bring in the wheat and feed it into the thrashing machine. Each farmer and helper drove their hay wagon out to the field where the helper would throw the bales onto the wagon using a pitchfork, and the driver would stack them into neat rows, layer by layer. When the wagon was full it was driven to the thrasher. I was in big demand with the cool water jug as the workers waited their turn to pull up and start throwing the bales into the machine.

The farmers' wives got together to put on the Thrashing Dinner, a big potluck meal. Grandma's specialty was fresh green peas. It was also Grandpa's favorite dish. All the other farmers and their wives knew this as a fact. This summer Grandma got Grandpa to one side and said, "Now, John, I know you like my green peas, but when the dish comes to you, take it easy so the dish will go around to everyone."

When the peas got to Grandpa, all eyes were watching. They all knew how much Grandpa like Grandma's fresh green peas. Grandpa majestically picked up his knife and placed one pea on his plate, then passed the dish on. Everyone smiled and then laughed as it was obvious Grandma had spoken to Grandpa in advance.

My grandparents didn't have any money to pay me for my labors that summer. They didn't have to. My pay was getting to know them better and stretching out a helping hand when one was needed.

Dishwasher
by Don Huling

WHEN I GOT back to La Salle in the summer of 1941, I was almost broke and needed a job in a hurry. Pork tenderloins were still fifteen cents at The Igloo. That's where Lindy and I headed on our first date.

The next day I went down to the unemployment office and told Mrs. Malone I'd take any job she had available.

"How about a dishwasher's job?" she said.

"I'll take it," I said as I headed out the door for the Vendom Hotel.

The Vendom Hotel was on the south side of First Street between Gooding and Wright Streets. The proprietor of the restaurant was a Greek fellow named George. When I arrived about 3:00 P.M. he told me to go home and change clothes and come back about 7:00 P.M. when the day shift dishwasher got off. They needed someone to wash dishes that night.

When I returned at 7:00 and went back into the kitchen, I couldn't believe my eyes. Every dish the restaurant owned was dirty! The day dishwasher had gotten drunk and hadn't washed a dish all day!

Well, nothing to do but get started. I figured I had helped Mom and Lindy dry dishes, but washing and drying took some figuring out. I finally worked out a system of washing ten cups, saucers, plates, knives, forks, and spoons to keep ahead of the waitresses, who had been doing their own dishes all day as they served up the food. I let the batch drain; then I wiped them dry with towels that were provided. I was ahead of the girls in half an hour, but with still a mountain of dishes to wash and dry. I kept at it all night.

In the morning, George came back to the kitchen and did a double take! Everything was clean and stacked up nice

Vendom Hotel, LaSalle

and neat. He disappeared for about a half-hour. When he came back he said, "Don, you're fired!"

I did the double take this time.

"Wally Formhals needs a good hard worker," George said, "and I told him I'd send you over. You're too good to be a dishwasher!"

Jobs of the Past We May Never See Again
by Don Huling

I RAN ACROSS an article in the October 2002 issue of *Reminisce Extra*. One paragraph reads as follows:

"And how long has it been since you saw an usher in a movie theater? Ushering was a great job for a teenager. You earned money, wore a snazzy uniform, and got to see the movies free."

Other jobs of the past that are long gone are Western messenger boys, pinsetters in bowling alleys, milkmen, icemen, elevator operators, Fuller Brush men, and telephone switchboard operators.

In 1942, Gerald "Mouse" Faletti and I were the two ushers working at the Majestic Movie Theater located at Second and Gooding Streets in La Salle. Our main job was to usher people to their seats when the situation indicated help was needed. People who arrived after the house lights were turned down and the movie had started usually needed assistance, especially if the theater was nearly full. We carried a flashlight we shined behind us and in front of the patron until we reached a row with vacant seats. We would then turn around, face the patron, and inquire if this row was satisfactory. If they nodded approval and it became necessary for the person in the aisle seat to stand, we would very courteously say, "Excuse us, please," and the late moviegoer would enter the row.

A lot of the job consisted of crowd control. When popular movies such as *Gone With the Wind* were showing, it became necessary to go outside the theater lobby before the ticket office opened and help form the line to go west on Second Street. Of course, we ushers in our snazzy uniforms looked real official. Once the ticket operator opened her office window, an usher waited inside the theater to make sure everyone entering had a ticket, which we would tear in half, giving half back to the customer. The other half we placed into a bin, which was emptied each evening. The tickets were numbered and when a drawing was in progress, the customers were encouraged to save their stubs in case the other half saved by the theater would be drawn from the barrel.

A couple of University of Illinois law students got together to beat this drawing game. One was an usher like me, who would draw the winning stub from the barrel on Saturday night. Whoever had the matching half would win one hundred dollars. Well, the two law students got together and worked out a "foolproof" plan. The usher palmed the half that was to go into the barrel. On Saturday night, his buddy and co-conspirator was in the audience with the matching stub. When the usher reached into the barrel, he already had the winning half in his hand. When he handed the stub to the theater manager, who read off the stub number, the other guy was supposed to jump up and run forward to collect the hundred dollars. Only something went wrong, and that is how I happened to read about this scam in the *Reader's Digest* magazine. The overly eager law student jumped up before the winning number was read!

Another job the ushers performed was changing the marquee Saturday night if a new movie was scheduled to start on Sunday. We used black metal letters and numbers nine inches tall that slid into slots on the marquee. It was about ten feet above the sidewalk. This made it necessary to climb both sides of a tall metal ladder that two ushers could ascend at the same time.

Gerald "Mouse" Faletti

David Symond

One Saturday night as Mouse and I were changing the sign, Mouse came close to having a serious accident. We got out the ladder and took down the old sign as fast as we could, then started up both sides with the new sign we had assembled earlier. Mouse lost his balance with his arms full of nine-inch metal letters. They went flying. Sid Seaton was exiting the theater right at this moment and caught Mouse in mid-air. I can only imagine what would have happened if Mouse had landed on the concrete sidewalk. We learned to slow down and use one hand to hold on to the ladder after this incident.

The snazzy uniform caught the attention of one of my junior-college friends, Dave Symond. The uniform consisted of light blue bell-bottom trousers, a light blue short-waisted, wide-lapel, long-sleeve blouse with white cuffs, heavy white paper dickey and collar, topped off with a light blue bow tie. We wore only a cotton T-shirt under this handsome uniform. Three tux studs made the dickey look like formal wear.

Dave was dating a girl in Lindy's senior class. We both attended their senior class prom, which was a dress-up affair held at South Bluff Country Club. I remember Lindy wore a beautiful white evening gown, and I had a dark suit, a plain white shirt, and black bow tie. Dave asked me to get him a white paper dickey with three tux studs and paper collar that we used as part of our usher's uniform.

When Dave and his date showed up at the dance, he really looked cool. I wondered why I hadn't thought of dressing up like that. Well, as the evening wore on, I was thankful I hadn't tried this getup. The weather was hot, and as Dave started to perspire, the paper dickey and collar started to "melt." Before the dance was over, Dave was wearing only his bowtie and T-shirt!

Lindy's Formals
by Don Huling

LINDY'S AND MY house at 1201 Bucklin Avenue in La Salle had a large attic where we stored items we no longer had an immediate use for but didn't want to part with for sentimental reasons.

Among these items were the formal dresses Lindy had worn on different occasions. I was a senior when Lindy invited me to her junior prom. She and her mom, Teta, had taken the Rocket train to Chicago to go shopping at Marshall Field's. Lindy had received five dollars from her grandmother Henry, and she wanted to buy a formal for the dance. They found a little red dress that had inch-wide straps and a nice little jacket for over the shoulders that they bought for six dollars.

Teta

I bought a red rose corsage for her that didn't exactly match the dress, but Teta told her not to be too concerned with such a triviality. It was the thought behind the deed that mattered. We went to the dance and had a great time. We were going steady at this point in our lives. Lindy thought I was a shrew when I wouldn't let her take off the jacket and display her naked arms and shoulders. Why should I do that? I had a good thing going and didn't want to share her with anyone. Our daughter Vickyle and granddaughter Corianne had fun modeling this dress in later years.

My senior prom was held out at Starved Rock State Park in the pavilion that no longer exists. We think Jug Horner's Band played for the dance. Jug was in Lindy's class, and the band was made up of her classmates. Lindy bought a blue-and-white cotton formal for this dance. We kept it in the attic for many years.

The nicest formal was the one Lindy wore to her senior prom in 1942. Teta had gone downtown to Blakley's Department Store and had returned with a dress that made Lindy cry when she saw it. It was an inexpensive mustard yellow with long sleeves, a short waistband, and buttons on the sleeves.

Lindy's father, Glenn, came to her rescue. Glenn liked nice clothes and agreed with Lindy that this yellow dress just wouldn't do. So he had Teta take Lindy back downtown to Blakley's. They came home with the nicest formal I've ever seen. It wasn't cheap—it cost twenty-five dollars, which was a lot of money at that time. It was white net with gold sequins and drop shoulders. I did a double take when I picked her up that evening to take her out to South Bluff Country Club.

My brother Paul didn't have a date for his senior prom. I was in the service, and Lindy was home from California, so it worked out just right that Paul should invite his sister-in-law to his dance. She didn't want to look matronly for the occasion and wore a navy-blue polka-dot skirt with white top.

I mailed this story to Paul, and on April 6, 2004, I got this reply:

Lindy in her red formal

> The way I remember taking Lindy to a formal dance is this: It was my junior year in high school (not my senior year as I was in the navy). You, Don, sent me five dollars when I told you by letter I could ask Lindy to go to the prom with me. Deal! One had to register with Miss Zimmerman, the high-school math teacher I had at the time, to attend the prom. When she asked me who my date would be, I said, "Ah, uh, um, Mrs. Huling."
>
> "What?" she said. "Speak up, Paul."
>
> "MRS. HULING," I said quite boldly so all around the room could hear.
>
> "OK, be serious. Who are you taking to the prom?"
>
> "Mrs. Huling, my brother's wife," I responded.
>
> Miss Zimmerman smiled quite broadly and announced to those who could hear how nice it was and that I was a nice boy to do that. GUSH.
>
> Lindy and I had a good time dancing and went to The Igloo after the dance. Then I wrote you about it, knowing how much you wish it could have been you.
>
> Bro Paul

Paul wasn't the only brother who got to take Lindy dancing. John invited Lindy to the Christmas dance that was held in the Hotel Kaskaskia. Lindy wore the white dress with the gold sequins and drop shoulders. This dance was open to the public, and John and Lindy saw a lot of people they were acquainted with. They knew Lindy and I had married quite young and that I was away in the service. John introduced Lindy as Mrs. Huling and left it at that—never explaining that he was her brother-in-law.

After the dance a lot of the young people headed to their favorite hangout—The Igloo. The place was crowded so John and Lindy sat out front on the bar stools where everyone who came into the place saw them sitting together. Lindy still laughs when she thinks of the stir they caused by being seen together. She—a married woman—out dancing with this good-looking fellow who had been away to forestry school out in Ames, Iowa, that they had not been introduced to. John was aware of the fuss they were causing but refused to tell the kids who he was.

Another formal that hung up in the attic was one we had acquired from a friend of the Marshalls—a Mrs. Sauer. Vickyle wore this dress with a large-brimmed hat in the play *I Do, I Do* for the number "Flaming Agnes." The show was directed by Mr. Robert Manahan.

Lunch at the Igloo

DO YOU KNOW what a shill is? I knew by the time I entered high school, because gambling was rampant and shills were used by gambling houses as well as by customers who thought they could out-shill the gambling house shills.

A shill is a person who tries to team up with another

person—or persons—to cheat an unsuspecting person and thus take him for a bundle of money. A card dealer may have marked cards, and the shill, appearing to be a customer but in reality working with the dealer, knows how to read the cards. The shill encourages the unsuspecting gambler to up the ante, knowing he, the shill, will have better hands. Knowledgeable, suspicious customers often ask for a new deck of cards while gambling, but the house and the shill, working together, have various was of overcoming this obstacle.

Before I continue, I should tell you I know about shills by being told, not by participating.

In La Salle there were many times during my youth that the police could not seem to solve gambling-related crimes. The word on the street was that the local underworld often settled accounts using violent means, and the police did little to solve the crimes because the sheriff had usurped their authority. A "retired" La Salle County sheriff told me a sheriff could retire after four years of service. In fact, he said, four years was all he was allowed to hold that job.

One "suicide" in my neighborhood, Doc Moran, had treated

a Chicago hood for a gunshot wound, but drank too much and talked too much. They put his feet in a bucket of cement, let it harden, then drove him and his car into the Illinois River.

At the place where I worked, my lunch hour was from eleven until twelve so there would be someone to take care of business during the hour of twelve to one when everyone else took off.

I was almost always the first customer of the day at the place where I ate. I usually picked the newspaper off the stoop and walked past the jukebox, removing the back cover to turn it on, then flicking all necessary buttons to make it play at least an hour without the necessity of paying a nickel per tune. For a couple of years after the Mafia took over jukeboxes in La Salle-Peru, Louie was told he would receive no service on his old one and would have to buy a new one from "them." So I serviced it for Louie.

This place was a regular hangout for many young people. The owner, Louie Mazzorana, had been a streetcar driver until the company bought buses; then he drove buses. He was a favorite driver for the high-school kids who rode his bus after school. At the end of the line he would have a few minutes to wait before driving his next round and he observed that a deserted streetcar turnaround would make a good location for a drive-in. He thought high-school kids needed a place where they could socialize under his observation. He bought the lot and built a very small place he called The Igloo, because of its size. His specialty became breaded pork tenderloin sandwiches, French fries, and milk shakes. It was such a success, he tripled its size just a few years later.

One morning I arrived to find the door locked and no newspaper to pick up. Louie opened the door and whispered, "Am I ever glad to see you. . . ." He signaled for me to come

Jack Harker, one of the first carhops at The Igloo. He wrote the poem "Pat." A copy hangs on the wall inside the Igloo.

PAT

Tonight I have the pleasure
of presenting someone who
is really very special,
one of God's chosen few.

She was always in the kitchen,
cooking porks and bar-b-q,
and Louie ran the counter
of the famous Igloo.

Her name is Pat, our guest of honor,
a very special gal indeed;
with grace and charm abounding
she filled a special need.

For those that worked for Louie
and those that ordered food,
her smile was a thing of beauty
and her manner never rude.

And Pat, you're still that charming lady
that I worked with long ago,
and that smile is still a beauty,
for it has that charming glow.

In heaven there's many mansions
and there's one there with your name.
It was reserved by Louie.
He's impatient—still the same.

Oh yes, there'll be an Igloo,
and Heaven will be blessed
by your presence—with no apron.
This time you'll be God's guest.

by Jack Harker
Class of '42

in and be quiet. He looked rough, no shave, haggard, tired. Inside were three men sitting at a table where it was apparent they had been playing cards all night.

There was grumbling among the three men; they did not like my presence. They argued with Louie that I wouldn't cause them any trouble and they could finish the hand being played. But Louie refused to cooperate, said they had agreed to play until the first customer arrived, and shuffled his cards into the deck on the table. The game was over.

I knew one of these three men. He lived at the southwest corner of Sixth and Joliet Streets in the cream-colored house with the large porch. I think he and his brothers made counterfeit money. He was my sister Alice's age, about ten years older than me. He had been in trouble with the law and was a gambler associated with other gamblers.

Reluctantly the three men left. It was then that Louie told the cook and me what had happened.

These men, who had always seemed friendly, came in as Louie was closing and asked if he wouldn't join them in a friendly poker game. Why not? was his response. The men knew he was tired after his fourteen- to sixteen-hour work-day and said he could quit when he was ready. But that's not what happened. . . .

Louie soon learned that one man was in total control of the others, who were his shills. The man in control wanted all of the owner's money, not just a little. They became mean. They played dirty. They threatened. They refused to produce new decks of cards, so the owner finally produced some from behind his counter. (They kept their used cards.) Trapped in this situation, Louie convinced them to stop playing when the first customer arrived.

The hand I broke in on was high stakes—about all Louie had, he said. By not playing that hand, he had broken even.

Yes, he was glad to see me, and he bought me my lunch that day.

Trick or Treat?

IT WAS A dark October night. The year was about 1941. What did boys do when it was autumn, the night was warm, and Halloween was in the air? Well, in a small town, some of us thought of things to do to get into mischief (without being malicious). Sometimes our judgment wasn't perfect. For us to throw a rotten tomato on someone's porch was about as trouble-some as we wanted to be, but that wasn't much fun because we ran so far so fast we never knew if the tomatoes hit the mark.

On this particular night, Tyler, Ezzie, and I had some-how gotten together and decided to terrorize our area of town, but we needed some new idea, something unique, a new challenge!

That's when Ty announced, "Let's trick-or-treat!"

"What's that?" was Ezzie's and my response.

"Don't you guys know what trick or treat is?" replied Ty.

So Ty explained to us this great new plan: we would knock on doors and not run when someone came to the door. (This was bold!) Instead of running, we would say "Trick or treat!" to whoever answered the door. That person would then be very happy to give us a treat! Very simple.

So we tried it out . . . very carefully. We thought our first client should be an easy touch, so we chose Tyler's grandfather, a nice old man. When the porch light came on, Ty stood way back (so as not to be recognized, he later told us). "Trick or treat" was Ezzie's and my greeting when Grandpa Goodman opened the door.

"What do you mean by that?" he asked.

"Well, if you don't give us a treat, we'll give you a trick," one of us said, somewhat hesitantly.

"What are you, a bunch of extortionists?" shouted Mr. Goodman as he swung open the door and jumped out.

Ezzie and I were gone! We cleared the seven steps to the sidewalk in one leap and ran for it! Ty was yelling, "Grandpa, Grandpa, it's me, Tyler!" as the old man reached for him.

Hey, this was fun! The old adrenalin really got a charge over this experience! Well, Grandpa took it all as a good joke,

Paul Huling

Tyler Goodman

Robert Esmond

invited us in, and fed us apples. As we left, we congratulated ourselves over our success. This was better than tricks!

Next we went to the Seatons, my next-door neighbors. We were a little more deliberate how we announced trick or treat and what it meant. When Mrs. Seaton recognized us, she took us right in. We ate apples.

Then we tried Ezzie's grandparents on up the street and enjoyed more apples there. We were on a roll!

By the time we got to the house next-door to Tyler's, my pockets were as full of apples as my stomach. We had decided to keep going from house to house till we got something besides apples, but had had no luck so far. Apples were all we got.

As we stood under the streetlight by Ty's house, the town police car rolled up to a stop. We didn't run (like guilty kids would); we just stood there. Then a policeman got out of the car and approached us like we were about to be handcuffed! We were a bit taken back by his mannerisms. Before he could say anything, Tyler threw up.

"What's going on here? What's wrong with him? Who are you? Where do you live? What's your name?" All these questions before we could think up the answers!

Somehow we got the story across that we were really good kids and that Ty had just eaten too many apples.

"Where'd you get 'em?" he asked. So we told him. He laughed. And laughed! Poor Tyler was puking apples, and the policeman just laughed.

Then he left, but I think I heard him ask one more question as he was driving off: "Who got tricked?"

⁂   ⁂   ⁂

PART IV

WAR YEARS AND BEYOND

The War

Sunday, December 7, 1941

I was handpicking popcorn in a field about four miles from town. Tom, the farm boy I was visiting for the weekend, heard the sirens first. I was used to them, being a town dweller, but soon realized Tom was right, there was something big happening to keep the sirens going so long. As we went on picking corn, I saw a familiar car driving down the nearby gravel road. It was my dad. It seemed early for him to come, so Tom and I quit picking and walked the half-mile back to the farmhouse, carrying our corn.

When we arrived at the gate, my dad was talking to Tom's dad. As we approached them, both men looked at us as though something grave had happened, and it would not be easy for them to tell us about it.

Neither Tom nor I realized that the day of infamy, Pearl Harbor Day, would greatly affect our lives, but our fathers knew. They seemed to study us closely as they told us the news.

I usually stayed at my friend Tom's farm until after a supper consisting of popcorn popped in salty churned butter, served with fresh cows' milk, but this Sunday Mom and Dad wanted the family together. That's why Dad had arrived so early to pick me up.

My mom had a tendency to fidget with her hands when she was nervous, and this night, at the dinner table, she tried not to, but the looks she gave each of her three sons revealed she was trying to suppress some deep emotion.

We listened to the radio as we sat at the dinner table. That was not normal. We—the father and sons, that is— talked about the war. Don was seventeen, would soon be eighteen; John had just turned sixteen, and I would turn fifteen in a few months. Mother left the room.

It was not apparent to me at the time, but later I realized I was no longer a boy in my mother's eyes. She knew that, from the day the war started until it ended, this family would prepare, and do, all we could for the war effort.

Mom was a club woman, in great demand. She organized well, delegated well, and was highly respected as a leader. Within months, she fulfilled all obligations to her clubs, then went to work in a munitions plant fifty miles from home, working swing shifts. Her days off were the eight extra hours she got when she changed shifts. When the regular driver's car broke down and needed repairs, Mom drove our car. She seemed to thrive on keeping busy.

Don was quickly drafted after completing a year of junior college. He was in the Air Corps. John tried to enlist in the Air Corps after high school. He knew he had a heart murmur and hoped he could slip through the physical, but a sharp doctor detected the defect.

Now mother had two purposes to work for her boys: one was to help with their education during and after the war, and the other to do all she could to shorten the war.

The war affected my grandparents, too. They were short of help for the work on their farm in Ohio. When summer came, my brother John and I boarded a train, loaded with our bicycles, and went to help them.

Grandfather was in his eighties, and Grandmother had very poor knees. Both had poor eyesight. Yet with the help of one hired man who lived with them, they carried on as best they could.

The Great Depression had hit the farm quite hard, and they would never fully recover; they had no tractor, just two horses, and 140 acres to farm. I raised a hundred chickens each summer so they could have chicken and eggs all year. They looked forward to having John and me on the farm.

One thing it meant for them was the use of our ration coupon books. The books enabled them to obtain more coffee and sugar for the summer. With the extra sugar, Grandmother canned blackberries that John and I picked on days we were not making the hay that fed the cattle all winter.

It was tough for my grandparents to keep on farming, but they never considered retiring and cooperated every way they could with the war effort.

My high-school classmates of '45 were freshmen when the war began. The European war ended just before graduation; many of us were already in the service. The Japanese war ended after graduation. During our high-school years, we had learned to cope with war in unique ways.

The girls learned how to say good-bye. They said good-bye to their fathers, who, in many cases, dusted off their old uniforms of war, or went away from home to work for the war effort, or worked such long hours there wasn't much time for association with their families. They learned to say good-bye to older brothers who were drafted or enlisted.

When a family sent someone to war, a flag with a star would appear in a window. Sometimes the flag would have two or three stars—a star for each person serving. These were flown with pride. And then sometimes—too often—the flag would bear a gold star, meaning a son or father or sometimes an older sister would not be coming home.

Boyfriends were a problem for girls my age. How many pen pals could a girl manage? How many soldiers and sailors did they want to encourage to continue a relationship when they came home on leave or weekend passes? Girls also had to learn about Dear John letters, letters written to close a relationship from far away.

When we were freshmen, girls my age dated older guys, because we boys were certainly not as mature as the girls. But by our senior year, the girls were saying good-byes again, to classmates this time.

The girls who took jobs in war plants to make bombs and military equipment worked hard and long hours. For the girls, Rosie the Riveter was the poster most representative; it was a picture of a young woman in bib overalls, bandanna tied over her hair, holding a rivet gun. For the boys, it was the I Want You! poster of Uncle Sam, whose finger and eyes you could not escape from any angle.

Gasoline was rationed. New tires—not good ones—required a permit granted by a government agency. There were no new cars, only older ones being pampered to stay roadworthy for an indefinite length of time and unlimited miles. The speed limit was 45 mph. Shoes, sugar, canned goods, and coffee were all rationed. These things made life for teenagers different from other generations, but it never

LaSalle-Peru-Oglesby selectees. See page 254 for names.

More LaSalle-Peru-Oglesby selectees. See page 254 for names.

seemed we were sacrificing nearly as much as those who were serving in the armed forces.

Monday, December 8, 1941

The day after Pearl Harbor was bombed, I delivered my newspapers to customers who had somehow changed from the Saturday before, when I had last delivered their papers. Someone at nearly every house on my route greeted me at the door to receive the paper, rather than picking it up off the porch later. Very few spoke to me as they stared at the newspaper I was handing them; it was as though they were trying to read the paper as it passed from my hand to theirs, and that maybe, just maybe, the headlines would say, Pearl Harbor a Hoax and not WAR.

What the newspapers did say was how many men had shown up that Monday morning at the post office to sign up for active duty in the armed forces: old men, fathers, fathers and sons—and sons, lots of sons.

By Tuesday, December 9, President Roosevelt had some-what calmed the nation from fear of imminent attack and had done his best to inspire the nation to give as much effort as possible to shortening the duration of the war.

School quickly changed. The futures my friends and I had expected to be earned in years to come were replaced by futures that were anxious to grab us. There was pressure to hurry up and grow up! We were needed to fill a uniform or we were needed for a new war-effort job if we would just quit school at age sixteen and go to work for the war. The pay would be better than what many fathers made at their old insecure jobs that they had labored so long to hang on to throughout the Great Depression. At age sixteen, many of my classmates left school for jobs.

Teachers enlisted in the armed forces, farmers enlisted, factory workers enlisted, clergy enlisted. Older boys did not exist; they were men in uniform, or doing men's work for long hours in the war effort. Boys like me, who could have quit to earn what was then a lot of money, were encouraged by our parents to stay in school. As we grew older, sixteen and seventeen, we were treated more like college-age men than teenage boys. Some of these boys grew up too fast, taking on responsibilities or lifestyles they were not mature enough to handle.

The pace of the war increased. It was big news in the local newspaper when a contingent of draftees gathered at the train depot to say their sad good-byes to families and sweethearts. As the war continued, the send-offs became less and less of a big deal. By the time my classmates and I came of age to serve, there was still some sadness expressed as our time came to leave, but we were probably the most well-adjusted recruits World War II had ever seen; our entire youth had been lived with the expectation we would serve and give our lives to our country, if need be. Older servicemen loved to see our arrival into service; it meant a stronger military because we were ready.

My classmates and I were among the last ones to enter the service before the enemy surrendered, and we were the last ones out when the war ended. Not surprisingly, some of my friends chose military careers.

Being the last ones out of service gave us a good opportunity to slow down the race to act as mature as possible and to plan our lives for a brighter, long-range future, one that extended beyond the next few weeks—or even days.

Those of us who lived through the war had a world full of opportunities ahead of us. We did pretty well. But now, we worry about how stupid it would be for the world ever to go to war again. . . . On that, we have not been outspoken enough.

Gas Station Attendant

I CAN REMEMBER my dad, in the late 1930s, driving past gas stations that sold gasoline at seven gallons for a dollar. It was common for gas stations to have price wars. One reason he might have driven past those stations was that in those days, cheap gas was likely to be inferior.

When Phillips Petroleum introduced Phillips 66 gasoline to the market, the name was intended to indicate that the gas octane rating was 66. That was high enough octane for some airplanes of the era.

This guaranteed octane rating provided an impressive sales pitch. At other stations, the octane rating was unknown to the customer. Some of that seven-gallons-a-dollar gasoline made car engines knock terribly during acceleration, and carbon deposits accumulated in the engines, making the knocking even worse.

By the time I was old enough to work at a gas station, during World War II, gasoline was twenty cents a gallon, and it was rationed. If a car had an A sticker on the windshield, the owner was entitled to four gallons of gas per week. Usually the person driving the vehicle wanted maximum mileage, so the most expensive gasoline with the highest octane rating became the best seller. It was called premium, ethyl, or high-test, as compared to regular, the lower-octane gas.

Working at a gas station was fun, but there was quite a bit more to it than what we expect when we drive up to an unattended gas pump today.

I was trained to greet the customer with a friendly smile before the engine shut off. Adding the gasoline required one to stand at the car and hold the nozzle, as there was no automated shut-off. Besides, very few people filled their tanks, for a number of reasons. Many cars needed oil added to the engine every one hundred miles or so. Therefore, enough gas was purchased to have the car go about one hundred miles. A car in good shape might go on two dollars worth of gas before needing oil. In 1944, it was exceptional if a car ran an entire tank full of gasoline and did not need at least one quart of oil.

After standing beside the car to add gasoline, I was expected to check the oil, clean the windshield, check the water level in the radiator, and check the tire pressure, unless the driver assured me that it was not necessary. Weather was never a problem. I dressed for rain, snow, sleet, or the heat of the day. The driver of the car usually did the same, because heaters were not very good and there were no air conditioners. Besides, one never knew when a flat tire would require mounting the spare.

Repairing flat tires was part of my job. I used tire irons to dismount a tire from the rim; there were no machines then to do this. Tires were like gold during the war, so every effort was made to reuse them. If the sidewall had a break, a boot (a large, thick patch) was placed over the break on the inside of the tire. This, of course, made the tire out-of-round, which made for a bumpy ride on smooth surfaces. If the car could go the speed limit, 45 mph, it was a good tire.

All tires used inner tubes. During the war, inner tubes were made of S-3, an early synthetic compound. When an S-3 inner tube developed a slow leak, one had to be careful about inflating the tube to find the leak. More than one attendant, including myself, added air to an S-3 tube to locate a leak, only to have the inner tube pop and the powder inside explode in a white cloud. I once applied fourteen small patches to a prewar inner tube rather than use a new S-3 tube.

Batteries back then didn't last very long, and I learned how to recognize when a battery was salvageable. I learned to shock and slow-charge a battery so that it might last another month or two (a handy bit of knowledge to have if the car was on a used-car lot, waiting to be sold).

New cars were almost impossible to purchase, but some dealers put a few of their 1942 models in storage. In early 1945, I helped clean up a new 1942 Chevrolet for delivery, and folks flocked around just to look at it in admiration.

Any car that could be coaxed to run was pampered and repaired, especially if the tires had a few miles worth of wear. One 1940 Cadillac that came in for regular servicing had over 300,000 miles on it the last time I serviced it! That owner had a rarely issued C sticker on his windshield. C coupons allowed owners to use more gas than A or B coupons did.

Once in a while there would be a lull in business. Then, if a friend dropped in, I could take a break and enjoy a Coca-Cola. But working at a gas station during World War II never got boring. In fact, it made me feel good that I was helping with the war effort.

The War Machine

M Y GRANDMOTHER CALLED a car a "machine." She did not want my grandfather to purchase such a folly, but if they owned such a machine, she could then ride in style. But first they would have to be able to afford one!

One summer day, George Bailey stopped by the farm to talk to Grandpa about threshing. George took care of the threshing machine that was owned by the co-op of farmers to which my grandfather belonged.

George kept looking at the clover in the nearby field. He said it looked like a fine clover. But Grandpa said it wasn't fine, because the alfalfa planted with the clover never had come up, which made the clover too rich to feed to his cattle. In fact, Grandpa said, the clover was a nuisance because it attracted bees.

With that, George got up, walked to the field, and proclaimed to Grandpa that he had a near fortune on his hands if he would let George thresh the clover to sell for seed.

Grandpa made more money on that field of clover than he had made on any crop before in his life! He bought a machine with the profits. The machine was a Patterson automobile. I know very little about its origins. I do know that it had six huge cylinders, each fitted with a primer cup that was filled with gasoline prior to cranking the engine by hand, as it had been built with no starter or battery.

Gramp's machine—the Patterson

My grandmother told me the car had very poor brakes. "It was great on Go," she said, "but slow on Whoa!" Then she told me about the day Grandpa cruised through the barn. Yes, he went right in the front door, through the barn, and out the back wall, ending up in the manure pile out back.

That did it! The fool thing went up on blocks for nearly twenty-five years! Grandpa never drove a car after that.

As kids, my brothers and I played in the old Patterson, pretending we were cruising down the road. Because the wheels were off the ground, we could steer it wildly as we dodged imaginary obstacles to win imaginary races. Although the cloth top was thick with chaff and dust and the leather-tufted seats had lost their luster, we sure did enjoy our pretend times in it.

About this time, I turned fourteen and lifted the hood. Wow! What an engine! It looked to be half the length of the entire car! I asked about the primer cups, figured out where the gas, oil, and water went, and tried the crank one day when no one was around.

I told my brother John that next year, when we visited the farm, we should be able to start it up and run it around the pasture. But I wasn't clever enough. Two weeks before my brother and I were to spend the summer helping at the farm, my grandparents sold the old Patterson for five dollars. That broke my heart then—and still does!—but it was probably a very good decision.

Grandpa told me the old Patterson was on its way to help win World War II. I thought he meant it was going to be scrap metal, but later I learned that not all of it was junked.

About a week after arriving on the farm, John and I heard a new sound. It was a far-off noise, like a tractor working under load. Now and then we would hear pop, pop, pop, followed by the sound of an engine recovering its working speed under heavy load. We soon learned that the unmuffled sound was the old Patterson engine as it powered the sawmill in Rosewood, Ohio, about two miles from the farm. John and I had to see it, so we rode our bikes to the mill.

There, powering the huge saw blade, was the old Patterson engine, pulsating steadily at a low rpm as the saw blade easily screamed through logs, slicing them into lumber.

As it awaited the next pass at the log, the blade idled and the engine relaxed and purred. When the log reached the blade, the engine would pop, pop, pop, picking up the load of the blade without loss of rpm. With each pop, there shot from the exhaust port of the engine a swirling blue smoke ring. The first ring out would be pierced by a second ring, then a third.

John and I watched the operation most of that morning. We were joined by a few local farmers who came just to see the old Patterson blow smoke rings and saw lumber.

I had second thoughts about cranking up that engine myself after seeing it working to help the war effort. It was making lumber that would build things to help win the war.

A Three-Sentence Letter

I DON'T RECALL who told me, but it seemed a good idea at the time: it would impress the U.S. Navy recruiting officer, and be good for my future placement, if I provided letters of reference. So I obtained three letters.

One was from Mr. Dolan, my high-school superintendent, stating that I had obtained enough credits to graduate that June.

The second was from Mr. Dean, manager of the local J. C. Penney store, where I had had part-time employment.

The third was from Mr. Leonard Travis, my current part-time employer. Mr. Travis owned the Cadillac-La

Francis Dolan

Salle, Oldsmobile, and Chevrolet motor cars and trucks dealership.

The letter from Mr. Travis was only three sentences. As I read the letter now, I sometimes wonder if it was really about me, or was it a letter to me to help guide my future? Either way, it has served me well.

TO WHOM IT MAY CONCERN:

This is to advise that Mr. Paul Huling of La Salle has been in our mechanical service department about one year. During this time he has shown exceptional aptitude and loyalty. In addition to this he has a fine character, and will undoubtedly make good anything he undertakes.

Yours truly,
Travis Motor Company,
By Leonard Travis

As I ponder the part about aptitude, I recall how helpful it became later on in my career. On more than one occasion I was faced with firing individuals because they just didn't have the aptitudes to perform. But firing was not always necessary. I would asked each employee if he was happy with his work. The answer was no. In a short time these employees would leave the company. Without exception word came back that they were much happier in jobs better suited to their aptitudes.

Loyalty meant a lot to Mr. Travis, and I was rewarded, along with all his other employees, because of it. During World War II the only way the dealership made money was through the service department, as there were no new cars to sell and very few used cars. Mr. Travis paid himself a salary and shared profits with his employees. Even though I had worked only one summer vacation plus after school and Saturdays, I was included in his bonus plan. How could one not be loyal to such an organization? The old-timers could have made much more money working at defense plants, but loyalty had become a very strong bond.

Paul graduating

Why did Mr. Travis value loyalty so much? His most senior mechanic, the one I was assigned to, told me this history:

Mr. Travis went into business as a dealer of autos in 1911. There were not many cars on the road back then, and garages with really good service were scarce. As he built up a good reputation, he was doing quite well—until the Great Depression.

In those days, General Motors Corporation sent dealers cars they had not ordered, and the dealers were required to pay for them upon delivery. That could have ended the dealership except for a local banker and Mr. Travis's employees. The banker risked his career by loaning the dealership money. The employees, in an all-out effort to stay in business, each purchased a new car, and they paid for them with holdings from their meager paychecks. The dealership survived the Depression to become the largest GM dealership in the area. Mr. Travis knew about loyalty.

As he handed me my letter of recommendation, Mr. Travis told me he remembered a heavy snowfall a few years back when I had knocked on the door of his house and asked if my friend and I could shovel his long walks and driveway. He said we had done a good job. I had all but forgotten the incident except I remember my share of the earnings was about equal to a whole week's worth of my paper route pay.

The letter said I would undoubtedly make good at anything I undertook. This was a statement of confidence; I doubt if I have lived up to it entirely. However, that statement has provided me with courage—the courage to try harder—and the will to succeed in all things undertaken.

That three-sentence letter is very important to me.

Stinger

MY FIRST REAL memory of "Stinger" was the day he chased John Small. What impressed me was that Stinger was driving his father's 1941 Plymouth, and John was walking on the sidewalk! John won; he stood behind a tree. Stinger lost when the front tire blew out as he hit the curbing. I was further impressed by the loss of the tire because this incident occurred during World War II and the Goodyear diamond tread looked so new but was ruined! Stinger drove home on the flat, about two blocks, parked the car were he had found it, and let his dad "discover" it. Stinger's dad never suspected him because he was too young to drive. Stinger had borrowed the car to learn to drive.

Julius "Stinger" Springborn

A few weeks later, Stinger's dad had an accident with that beautiful burgundy-colored Plymouth, and the car was totaled.

Because of the war, the only car Stinger's dad could find was a 1937 Ford 60. Stinger couldn't wait to borrow this car. By now he was a slightly better driver but still didn't have a license. All went well until Stinger attempted to return the car to its parking spot in front of the house. Because the muffler was a little noisy, Stinger decided he would coast down the hill the last block from home, round the corner, stop in front, and silently slip away.

Well, it didn't quite work out that way. In the first place, Stinger turned off the ignition switch, removed the keys, and slipped them into his pocket. This locked the steering wheel on the 1937 Ford. To retrieve the keys from his pocket, Stinger had to take his foot off the brake pedal. Too late! The 1937 Ford also had mechanical brakes that didn't slow the car down enough. So Stinger parked the car where it came to rest, and that was on the front porch! His dad was sleeping on the couch—before the crash. Stinger's dad decided it was time to teach him to drive.

One night we went sledding in Peru, a couple of miles away. We parked at the top of the hill, sledded till we got cold, and started for home, which was behind us and up the hill. Stinger started down the hill, slid past the turn at the first block, slid some more on the ice we had all compacted with our sleds, missed the second chance at the next block, and assured us that in one more block he would have the skid under control, and we would turn either left, or right, at the next corner. We had to, because the next block was a tee intersection, and we couldn't go straight.

We almost made it, but the front wheel bent so badly as it hit the curb that all the way home that wheel didn't rotate if we were on ice, but it did rotate if we were on cinders. When it turned, we knew from the noise and smell that we would not make it home before wearing a hole in the tire. As there was no spare tire, we drove home using only icy side streets. The radiator overheated because of the stuck wheel, but Stinger made it home and parked it on the hill.

Next morning, his dad, not knowing the condition of the wheel, started down the hill, lost control on the ice, and hit the curb. He swore he wasn't going fast enough to do all that damage!

One night Stinger got permission to use the '37 Ford to go to a basketball game. On the way, he missed a stop sign because the lights on the Ford were so dim, and a huge truck ran over the Ford. Stinger wasn't hurt, nor were his two friends. In fact, Stinger faked a bad limp as he walked up to his dad to explain why the '37 Ford was junked.

Stinger's dad found an Oldsmobile next. He wanted something heavier and stronger. This 1938 Olds was a light blue. Looked nice. It was a wartime repaint, probably the only car in the world this exact color.

Stinger convinced his dad he'd better take the Olds out for a spin, to be sure he didn't have any hidden fears about driving since wrecking the Ford. Once again fate would have it that as we cruised around the winding, hilly curves of Westclox Park, the accelerator pedal became stuck.

At first we thought Stinger was just showing off the great power of the Oldsmobile. Then Stinger disappeared from view as he reached down to disengage the gas pedal. Our screams brought him back to driving position, and he got the thing headed straight again. So he kicked the gas pedal to release it, only it got stuck to the floor. Once again he grabbed it with his hand, but only produced the gas pedal! The linkage was still down there someplace!

Of course, by now the car was totally out of control and Stinger jammed the brake and clutch at the same time. It was then that we heard those loud knocking noises emerging from the engine as it roared at top speed.

We walked back to Stinger's house and waited while he told his dad about the car. We didn't know what to expect; Stinger's dad could get pretty mad. But Stinger shortly appeared, smiling! His dad hadn't paid for the car yet and wasn't about to. In fact, he never bought the car, decided to wait till after the war before he bought another. I'll bet I know why.

Bessie

BESSIE WAS THE name of my first automobile, a 1931 Model A Ford Tudor sedan. I owned that car for three years and drove it 60,000 miles at a cost of 1.8 cents per mile. I paid $125 for it in 1947 and sold it for $115. I drove it as far west as Ames, Iowa, and as far east as New York City, via Canada.

The asking price for Bessie was $350, but the gas station where Bessie was displayed for sale knew nothing about Model As, so Bessie quickly acted up and wouldn't run right. The last owner of Bessie had died. He had been a good friend of mine and had often let me drive Bessie, so I knew the car.

As Bessie sat for weeks with no buyer, I approached the sister of the previous owner and told her I could only afford $125, so if the price ever got that low I wanted a chance to buy her. About a week later she called, as she needed to settle the estate.

The guys at the gas station were mad when I went to pick up Bessie, as they claimed they had also wanted her. They were really mad when in about fifteen minutes I had her purring like a kitten because I had spent thirty-five cents for two new carburetor jets before arriving to pick her up. That was all that was wrong—she was ready to go.

It wasn't long after I bought her that a man approached me and told me he had owned Bessie before the war and had driven her 110,000 miles before he sold her.

Bessie

A few weeks later a young woman approached the car as I sat in it waiting for a friend. She asked me if there was a silver wings pin, awarded to World War II pilots, pinned above the mirror. There was, so I gave her the pin; her now-discharged boyfriend had wanted to save it. She told me Bessie had been her Green River Ordinance defense plant transportation throughout the war, that she had driven the car from 110,000 to 190,000 miles before she sold it to Eddy, the owner before me.

When I bought Bessie, the odometer said 20,000 miles, so that was really 220,000, to which I added 60,000 more. Model A's were good cars!

Because I worked for auto dealers during the three years I owned Bessie, I could purchase parts, like tires, wholesale. Junkyards had a fine supply of everything else I might need. I tried never to have Bessie on the road after sundown, and only twice did she have to be shut down more than a day.

Bessie would cruise all day at sixty miles per hour; her top speed was seventy. One day, returning home to Illinois from Michigan, I stopped to pick up a hitchhiker. He refused me, saying he would get a ride in a faster car. Three times I stopped as he got his short rides, and three times he refused. When I got to Angola, Indiana, where I turned off to head west to La Salle, there he was, standing along the road. We smiled as we waved.

One night after a basketball game, there was a group of students waiting to catch a bus to The Igloo at the far end of town, so to impress my girlfriend, because they were her close friends and she was with me, I asked if they didn't want a ride instead of taking the bus. They did, so ten more got in, making it twelve. There were only three of us in the front seat, though.

Now you may think that as a young, single male it would be quite a handicap to attract young beautiful women to a tin lizzie when other young men were sporting newer convertibles and the like with great success. But one day the most beautiful of all asked me if she could drive my car. I married her!

Miss Gertrude Reichter

"GERTIE." I REMEMBER her keeping me after class at LPO Junior College after giving me back my first test paper. She merely said to me, "See you after class! At my desk!"

My test paper said E, and E wasn't for excellence, so I figured Gertie was going to advise me to drop out of Economics 101 while the getting out wouldn't be too apparent on my record. No, that was not her advice.

When the class left—all but me—she said, "Sit!" like she would command a dog.

Gertrude Reichter

I sat, like an obedient dog. And who wouldn't! Gertie stood about six-two, weighed in at about 240, and was so shaped like a football player, the coach was forever trying to avoid being run over by her! Well, not really run over; "gathered up" would be more like it. Gertie didn't really have a crush on the coach, but she loved to intimidate him. He was only six-foot, also weighed about

"Butch" Nowack

240, only lower slung. When Gertie gathered him in, Butch (the coach) would turn deep maroon and was afraid to use his hands to pry her loose. Gertie would roar with laughter. Butch would go out of his way to avoid Gertie's territory in the halls.

"Don't you know anything about economics?" was Gertie's first remark to me; then without waiting for what would have been my negative answer, she said, "Tell me what you know about laissez-faire."

The answer I had written on the test said, "Buyer beware." Obviously Gertie wanted more than a two-word answer, so I told her something about free trade and maybe about monopolies, but then I just sort of recalled some of the things she had talked about that had not been in the textbook. As I talked, I realized she was taking in what she had said much better than what the text had said. After all, she had assigned us seventy-five to one hundred pages of text at every class, then talked about stuff not in the text throughout the class. I had figured the test was on the text; then I realized she was really testing me on what she had said. So I began to bring into my answer about laissez-faire anything that came to mind from what she had told us. I told her about Harry Truman, the stock market, the national debt, export tariffs, income taxes, and more about monopolies.

As I was taking a breath to start in again, she stopped me and said, "Fine, now you've got the idea. . . . Of course you just went ahead and answered all the rest of the questions on the test while you were at it, but just remember that when you're given a test where you can narrate, tell it all, and you're sure to hit on the answer as you go! Here, we'll change the E to C. . . . I'd have given you a B, except you made Harry Truman sound too good."

One day Gertie walked into the chorus practice room as we were singing "Deep River." Her room was across the hall. She heard us when her door was open. She announced to the director she was "ready to take it from the top" The choral director, being a rather short, thin man, and knowing how Gertie treated Butch, just said, "OK, from the top," and we started over with Gertie taking the solo. Our mouths would have fallen open, except they already were, when Gertie belted out the song in a strong, deep contralto voice that made our hair stand on end. When she finished, we applauded. She bowed, smiled, and left. We could never entice her to do it again.

I had Gertie for many other classes, as I was an economics major. I never had a problem taking tests in her class again. She got to know me pretty well. In fact one day she asked me if I would help her move from one apartment to another on a Saturday afternoon. She needed my car and someone else to help. I chose my friend Lyle. The move was no problem except getting her in and out of the front seat of my Model A Ford. When she got in, there was precious little space for Lyle and all the stuff we'd packed into the car.

All afternoon she kept asking me about my car until I though she probably wanted to buy it—but no, that was not it. She wanted to know if she could drive it. That's when Lyle and I learned she had driven tractors in her youth, but at about age sixty she had never driven a car. I sort of suggested in a roundabout way that the seats in my Ford were not adjustable backwards and she might not fit behind the steering wheel, otherwise we could teach her to drive. She seemed to accept that evaluation pretty well.

When all her belongings were in place in her new apartment, she asked us what to do about the bathtub. It seems that during Prohibition days someone had made bathtub something in the tub, and it had removed the enamel from the bottom. Lyle and I knew of some new finish, just made for painting metal and especially for bathroom fixtures, so we bought her a can and a brush, then gave her directions. By this time, Lyle and I thought we'd better leave before she came up with more problems.

About Tuesday, following the move to her new apartment, Gertie cornered Lyle and me and asked us how to remove paint. Beating around the bush a bit, we got her to disclose where the paint was that she wanted removed. It seemed that Gertie had figured it would take the entire can of paint to paint the tub so she just poured the entire contents into the tub and swished it around with the brush and pulled it up the sides. When it had dried—or so she thought it was dry because it was dry to the touch—she got in and sat down in a tub of hot water, only to find underneath the skin of dried paint was a pool of very wet paint. As Gertie tried to remove her large self from the tub, the skin coat had slid like a banana peel, and thus Gertie had completed the job of messing up the paint job and her entire lower body. Of course we fixed her tub, but Gertie was on her own for the rest of the mess.

Then one day Gertie cornered Lyle and me again and asked if we'd teach her how to drive. Once again we hemmed and hawed. Then she told us she had just bought a brand-new Buick and had had it delivered to her parking garage and wanted to take it for a drive. Luckily, I was working a part-time job, so Lyle had the honor of taking Gertie out for her first lesson. Gertie failed. Lyle finally gave up teaching. He drove her around and recommended that she take driver's ed from the local high school. This she did.

It so happened that the driver's ed car was sponsored by the Pontiac dealership where I worked part-time. We had prepared double pedals for the clutch and the brakes, so the driving instructor could take over the controls if necessary. (In those days all driver's ed classes required a car with standard transmission.)

Well, Gertie got off to a pretty bad start on her first lesson. It seems she had finally achieved a good enough takeoff to find herself cruising down the street, when she decided to make a turn at the next corner without telling the instructor. So she slammed on the brakes, which caused the instructor to brace himself. In so doing, his feet went forward against the floorboard at the same time Gertie decided to press the clutch pedal.

Of course, she also depressed the clutch on his side because the pedals were connected. Little did she know the reason the clutch would not fully depress was because the instructor's feet were under the pedal. He screamed in pain. . . . She pressed in response.

Gertie proudly told Lyle and me that on her very first driver's lesson she had the opportunity to drive solo all the way to the emergency room of the hospital! As they hauled off the instructor on a stretcher, he gave orders that she was not to drive the car back to the school alone.

What I would like to ask Gertie is how much fun she's having in heaven. She sure was a fun person here on earth.

New Year's Hitchhikers

JANUARY 1, 1948, WAS bitterly cold as I left La Salle, Illinois, to drive to Flint, Michigan. It would be hours before the sun came up. I wore a peacoat from my navy service, my black navy watch cap, and galoshes in an attempt to ward off the below-zero reading on the thermometer.

My car Model A was not warm, even with a manifold heater. I drove the first hundred of nearly four hundred miles I would drive that day in darkness.

There was very little traffic on U.S. Routes 6 and 20 as I traveled east. I was bored, lonely, and tired from staying up past midnight with my girl to bring in the New Year.

I wasn't long into Indiana before I approached two young men hitchhiking, shivering as they huddled against the cold wind. I stopped to give them a lift, telling them both to get in the front seat in order to be near the hole in the firewall where the heat from the manifold entered the car.

I was on my way to General Motors Institute (now known as Kettering University). They were hitchhiking to Hillsdale College in Hillsdale, Michigan.

With three of us in the front seat, it was much warmer. What little heat drifted in from the heater tended to stay up front, especially when the boys put their feet as close to the source of heat as possible. They were stiff with cold; I had been the first car to drive past them for ages, they said.

After about a half-hour, one of the boys let out a yell, saying the hair on his leg was burning! It wasn't, but he and the other fellow had put their feet so close to where the heat came out that the heat had finally penetrated the poor kid's leg, causing him to scream in surprise.

After that, we became quite warm as the two of them moved a little farther away from the heater.

Traffic was so light that there was no way I could put those fellows out in the cold as we came to the road to Hillsdale. So I drove the extra miles out of my way to deliver them to Old Main on their campus.

Nineteen-forty-eight wound up being a good year for me. I figured it was because I had started the year by doing a good deed for a couple of boys who really needed help.

Juliet
Remembered by Jean Huling

THE TELEPHONE RANG early Monday morning, back in the 1960s.

"Would you be willing to help me study the music for my voice lessons?" It was Juliet, a black woman I'd met two years before when she sang at our church, where I was the organist.

"Sure," I answered, "but is this because of the sermon yesterday?" Juliet had again been our vocalist, and the sermon we both heard was a powerful one titled "Unlimited Horizons." Our minister's point was to "get out there today and do what you have been putting off, things you know God wants you to do." Already that morning his wife had called me to start piano lessons, and it had also moved me to place an order to a music store for some ragtime piano pieces (something I had always wanted to play).

"Yes, it was that sermon," Juliet answered. "I've decided to really concentrate on my voice."

With my classical music training, I knew I was suited for the job. Juliet had been cleaning houses to pay for voice lessons. Life was hard for her; she had to support her ten children because her husband was unable to work due to a construction accident. She had no car, so at first she rode the bus to our town. However, several times she was stopped by the police when she walked the three blocks from the bus stop to our house. She was in tears. Apparently some neighbors had complained that a Negro woman was walking down the street of our small, white farm town. Soon I was picking her up once a week, bringing her to my house to practice.

Our friendship was mutual. Although I helped her for free, she often stayed late to help me with household chores or brought baked goodies for us. Our children became acquainted with hers. We began working several days a week on her music when I took a job as an organist at an integrated church where she was the soprano soloist.

Soon Juliet was performing classical concerts, and paying me to be her accompanist. We rejoiced when she was hired for a concert tour of Sweden. Next, she went to Germany seven times for the U.S. Army Chaplains, singing for the troops.

When my husband was transferred to Brazil in the mid '70s, I hated to leave her and our music. But on our first home leave she threw us a big party at her home. We convinced her to come to Brazil to visit, and she performed at

Juliet King

the Brazilian-American Cultural Union, at several churches and on radio and TV, and sang spirituals to young people. By this time I was using my ragtime piano with a band in Brazil, and she performed with us as well.

Forty years later we are still friends. Twice she has flown from Illinois to Ohio to sing and speak at our church. When some of our band members decided to do a church service of spirituals, she flew out again. Her carry-on baggage that trip included the makings for an entire dinner she fixed for the band after church!

Juliet continues to sing around the world. Even the Pope has heard her sing! I feel blessed to know her.

Chester
Remembered by Paul and Jean Huling

DRIVING THROUGH APPALACHIA on vacation in 1963, we finally saw the kind of chair Jean had been hunting. It had a bark seat and "mule-ear" posts. We had seen this kind on porches, but never for sale. An old sign, written in a form of antiquated English, said something about furniture:

CORNETT CHAIRES
WEY CAN MAK INEYTHIN
ARE HEIT CANT B MAD

"Please stop the car," Jean asked. Our children were glad for a break anyway, due to dizziness from the circuitous mountain roads in Kentucky.

Paul: I got out to investigate while Jean and the kids stayed in the car. Up close, the chair was a child-size rocker. A man in big overalls came from behind a large kettle that was simmering.

Jean: moonshine?

Paul: No, steaming wood to form it into a shape.

"Hit's a good chire," the man in overalls said.

"Do you have any bigger ones?" I asked.

"Hit's plenty big," he said. Amazingly, he plunked himself into the little chair and began to rock. I guess it was the bib overalls that made him look huge, or maybe the beard, filled with wood shavings and other items.

The chair was no longer bright; in coal territory, new wood loses its luster in a short time. But what a beautiful piece of craftsmanship! I bought it for Chester's asking price: $9.00.

Jean: The children and I tentatively got out of the car. The house was gray tarpaper, built on a slag pile that wouldn't grow grass. While Paul was talking to Chester, we saw a dirty woman, dressed in rags, sidle out the back door. She was carrying a naked baby, and soon two more filthy toddlers came outside to cling to her legs. One of the children was drinking condensed milk from a can. The only girl looked to be about 8 years old. She sat down and rocked in the rocker we had just bought. There were several larger boys hanging around, but we soon realized that they were profoundly retarded and unable to speak.

Paul: I thought my family would be happy with the chair when I loaded it onto the back of the station wagon. But instead they were all in tears! The children had never encountered poverty like this before. What could we do, they asked? We didn't know these people, and for all we knew, maybe everyone this far back in the hills could live this way if they wanted to.

Here was a man with the talent to craft beautiful things, but he was pitifully underemployed. How could he possibly make a living? That night our family talked about how to help.

Next day we returned to Chester's place and ordered four kitchen chairs like the ones he had on his porch. I learned that Chester and his family lived on a $50 a month pension from the government—and whatever he could earn from selling chairs. We paid him half in advance, the balance on receipt . . . never knowing if he would finish them. It meant

Paul & Chester

scheduling a return visit to Kentucky, but the entire family wanted to do this. I soon found out why.

Our girls gathered up dolls, the boys old toys, my wife some dresses, and I found a few old carpenter tools handed down from my grandfather. Our beautiful chairs were ready on time, and we had new friends.

Over the period of a few years, we ordered many tables and chairs. Also some of our friends bought from Chester. But one winter Chester wrote and told us his family was hungry. He was in need of more sales and customers. Again we wondered how we could help from so far away.

While in Kentucky, we had always looked forward to the bi-weekly local newspaper. Reading it for a few weeks made one knowledgeable of many things in that area. So we called the editor about Chester's plight. She said that she and her husband would visit him that same day.

She called back the following day to say she had bought two walnut bookcases. (Chester had made them for a customer who failed to return to pick them up.) These bookcases fit perfectly, one on each side of the fireplace in her home. Just what she had always wanted! For her paper, she wrote a story about Chester. She obtained permission for him to set up sales on a busy street corner, whenever he had things to sell. When she told the mayor about our family, the mayor made us honorary citizens.

Chester was "on his feet." He made a chair for then-President Nixon and delivered it to him in Washington. He proudly showed us a picture of himself with Nixon.

The last time we saw Chester was in 1971. He had moved near Cincinnati where he had a job making furniture in the showroom of a furniture store. Here folks of all ages and walks of life could see, study, and purchase fine furniture, made by a true mountain craftsman.

Why Mailwomen Don't Wear Skirts

ONE BEAUTIFUL SPRING Sunday morning I was washing the car and watching the dog. With Gus the dachshund that's the way it was. He didn't watch you very often, you watched him, because if you didn't remind him where his yard was, he soon drifted away to others. Well, this day he was sniffing the lot line minding his own business when a mail truck pulled up near the mail deposit box that sat on the corner of our lot. A woman stepped out, a mailwoman, and she was dressed in her finest, brightest, brand-new, just-off-the-shelf, regulation U.S. Postal Service uniform—with skirt. She also carried the large leather mailbag into which she would place the contents of the mail deposit box.

Gus loved mail carriers. He would wait all morning so he could greet Lee, the mailman; they were great friends. Well, the mailwoman bent over and scooped up all the deposits in the mailbox, and just as she was about to slide them into the leather pouch, old Gus ran his nose up her skirt!

The next scene was awful. I hid behind the car, but peeked through the windows. The mail she had gathered was thrown upward and fluttered . . . mostly into the street. The shriek she let out seemed  to please Gus. So each time she bent over to pick up a letter—and there were many—Gus assumed it was a game in which he was to keep his cold nose in close contact with the mailwoman's undergarments.

I could no longer stand this! I sneaked into the house and asked my dear wife if she would mind calling Gus, as he seemed to think Lee had sent a special Sunday delivery just for him.

The letters never did get placed in the leather pouch. It was not a normal mail pickup. The letters were thrown into the mail truck through the open windows. Some looked rather damaged. I watched from inside the house.

Gus happily finished walking the perimeter of the lot. I finished washing the car. And evidently the mailwoman burned her skirt, because she never wore it again as far as I could tell.

Rags

I MISS RAGS. Rags was "my" dog. First he was other people's dog. He changed homes quite a few times his first year, before he became Jean and my family's dog for the next thirteen. But I think of him always as my dog because no one else could cut his hair.

Rags was blind most of his life. What an inspiration he was! He could have given up as a helpless invalid. He could have been overcome with fear. He could have become bored, mean, crabby, introverted. But he was none of these. Rags loved life.

The name Rags suited him well. First he was Rocky, named after a boxer character from a movie. That was a very fitting name; he was sort of a speedy klutz. He couldn't sit still. He was rowdy, feisty, jumpy, and chased horses. We altered his name to Rocky Rags, then to Rags. He looked like a bundle of stuff you'd dust with or sprinkle around on an oil spill. His hair grew fast and curly.

His first haircut took three days. As he sped past, I'd reach out with the scissors and try for a snip. It wasn't a very good haircut.

One day Rags leaped against the large plate-glass window in front of the house. We wondered why he hadn't seen it. A little later our doctor friend noticed his eyes were not right. It wasn't long before he lost both eyes. That was a very sad day.

Rags had never needed me before now. He had always displayed his independence without showing affection. After he became blind, Jean, my wife, sat and cried with him and assured him we could take care of him. He responded by taking care of us. He remained independent. And he became more affectionate. He could still be rowdy. He knew where he was and where he was going. He held his head high and marched forth. If he hit a wall or a tree, he either collapsed like an accordion or bounced off. Didn't complain. Didn't give up. He was the leader when we went for walks. Now he let me cut his hair in only two days.

When we told Rags who was at the door, he greeted each person according to his or her personality. He had many friends. He loved to announce every UPS delivery truck that went past the house. Other trucks didn't matter. Meter readers knew he knew they were present.

Rags taught me a lot about love. All dogs do, but Rags had a special message. When life is dark and doesn't look so good, there is a reserve from which can be drawn one's true self. If Rags felt sorry for himself, he never showed it. When I felt sorry for him, he couldn't comprehend why, thereby convincing me I was wrong. Like when we took him for rides in the car, he would look out the windows for horses. He knew he might see one, even though I thought I knew he couldn't.

I miss Rags. I'll bet he's in Dog Heaven, romping with a horse and waiting for me to cut his hair as he zips past.

Locked Out

A NEIGHBOR OF mine attended an auction in Middle-field, Ohio, one day last summer. He had absolutely no intention of bidding on one item that came up for sale, but when he heard what the guy next to him was going to do with the fifty rabbits coming up for bidding, it made him angry. So my neighbor opened the bid at ten cents apiece, just to force the other fellow to pay a little more to get them.

What my neighbor would do with fifty rabbits was not considered, he just didn't want that guy to get those rabbits without competition. Somewhere, this plan went haywire. The other guy had left the auction, and my neighbor became the proud owner of fifty rabbits for five dollars, total.

As he loaded them into his pickup truck and covered them over with a tarp, he got a good look at them. Each one was different! He didn't realize it at the time but each one was a rare breed; he had purchased someone's collection of fancy-bred *Oryctolagus cuniculus forma domestica* . . . translated, tame rabbits.

He had absolutely no problem at all as to what to do with them. The rabbits had been penned up in cages all their lives, so he would reverse their condition of solitude. Instead of being locked up all their lives he would lock them out by gifting them to Unionville. He set them free in our little community.

The first day I saw them, there were about twenty in his yard: white ones, black ones, black-and-white, brown-and-white, gray, fuzzy gray, long-eared, floppy-eared, spotted, green eyes, pink eyes, you name it. My first reaction, and I'm sure there were others who thought the same, only more so, was, "What have I had to drink lately that would cause me to see strange things?"

It didn't take long before they spread out. Most seem to have paired up and found territories in the back fields, backyards, under decks, or found refuge in a vacated dog house where feed and straw is provided by yet another neighbor.

We have a golden retriever, and we thought there would be no problem with rabbits in our yard. Besides, my wife didn't like rabbits . . . until "Fluffball" came to visit. Fluffy loved one of my wife's flower gardens and quickly disposed of it.

As we plotted on how to save the remaining gardens, along came "Florence," short for Florence Nightingale, who discovered the rhubarb, a rabbit delicacy we no longer have.

Our golden retriever has a very soft heart. Rabbits love him just like people love him, and he loves people . . . and rabbits; in fact he loves everything. Anyway, the two rabbits hopped up to him while he was outside peeing. This was very embarrassing to Gus, but curiosity turned to satisfaction as they became friends.

With my wife's flower gardens slowly disappearing, we decided the rabbits were hungry, so we offered Fluffball a carrot. Much to our amazement, he couldn't find it even when it was very near. Fluffball is blind in one eye and doesn't see well out of the other. But it wasn't long before Florence showed up to help him.

Fluffball, we learned from a rabbit book, is a gray Angora. His ears flop over his eyes and he looks like a half deflated soccer ball covered with fuzz. Florence Nightingale is a White Ermine Rex with beautiful white slick hair, pink eyes and nose. At first she only showed up in the yard at night . . . and I mean she really sort of glows at night. We call her Florence because she is the companion to Fluffball, and Nightingale was added because it fit her personality so well.

Now, the garden is very dormant, or gone, and my wife has become fond of these two free spirits. They visit us twice or more each day for cabbage and carrots and follow me, my wife, and the dog around the yard. They surprise people who come to see us, especially Fluffball. The general comment is, "What is that?" You see, Fluffball has not been combed or brushed to look like the pedigree he really is.

"He" is what we call Fluffball, "she" is what we call Florence, although we have no way of knowing their sexes . . . yet. The book says we may find out.

What is amazing about these two creatures is the care and companionship they share with each other. Florence will hop over to Fluffy, they touch noses, then Fluffy follows Flo to food we have put out. Flo does not wish to be touched, but she will place her carrot on my shoe if I stand nearby. Fluff doesn't really see me so I speak to him to draw him to food. They arrive together, spend their nights together in the front yard, and leave together to sleep all day.

One day a huge hawk landed in the maple tree just beyond the deck at the back of our house. The hawk swooped down and we never saw what it picked up. For two days after that we didn't see Fluffball and were sure he was gone. Then it snowed and we could spot Fluff against the white snow. Flo was invisible until I felt her nibbling on my pant cuff.

And that's the way it is. Each one of God's creatures has moments to stand out, each has moments to share. How wonderful it is that Fluff and Flo, who were most surely isolated in separate cages to keep their breed lines pure, have found happiness and freedom in God's world. It's great to see them free.

My wife, my dog, and I love these two rabbits. And, you know, everyone in Unionville seems pleased with our neighbor's investment.

❈   ❈   ❈

Latin I

ABOUT FIFTY YEARS after taking Latin I from Mr. Trobaugh, I had the opportunity to thank him for encouraging me to keep trying when the going seems rough. I told him he had been my favorite high-school teacher.

At the end of my freshman year he said to me, "Paul, don't sign up for Latin II." That alone would win him high favors from me, but he went on: "The reason you passed Latin I is because you never gave up; you'll never fail if you keep trying."

Earl Trobaugh made Latin I as interesting as he could. He told us stories, made fun of some Latin derivatives, and

Earl Trobaugh

often featured students by pointing out their finer points in a seemingly joking way. He built on our weaker points (Latin I for me) by featuring our strengths. He made an impression on my life, as well as encouraging me in my continuing education.

After I thanked Mr. Trobaugh, some fifty years after his influence on my life, he later told my mother-in-law that I was the only previous student who had thanked him or told him he had inspired a student's future. I'm so glad I had the chance to do that.

The story could end here except for other times in my life when Mr. Trobaugh's influence became apparent.

When I was nearing my eighteenth birthday and not yet out of high school, I joined the U.S. Navy. My summer and part-time job had been working for a car dealer. Cars were easier for me than Latin, so I had made good progress as a mechanic. Mr. Leonard Travis, the dealer, wrote a letter of recommendation for me in which he stated I would make good at anything I undertook. I wanted to show that letter to Mr. Trobaugh more than to the navy.

Years later I became depressed while working as an engineer; it seemed my job, my future, and the company were in turmoil. I was not happy. Then Jean, my wife, said to me, "Why don't you quit and find a job somewhere else?"

What a profound question to ask me. . . . I didn't quit! I didn't give up! Things turned around. I think she knew that would happen when she asked the question. Just as in Latin I, I could survive if I didn't give up.

So Mr. Trobaugh caught a spark and ignited it. Mr. Travis recognized a desire to succeed. And my dear wife knew the surest way to lift my doldrums was to suggest I give up.

What beautiful people have helped steer me through life!

But that is not the end of this story. In fact, there is a

Warren T. Robinson

beginning to this story that is very important. I had not intended to sign up for Latin I at all. But my childhood buddy and lifelong friend Tom Robinson examined my freshman schedule and suggested I needed Latin I as an additional course to prepare me for college. Years later he told me he felt badly about influencing me to jump into something that was truly over my head. Little did he realize I needed that Latin I for preparing for life! And for that I thank him over and over again.

❋　　　❋　　　❋

APPENDIX

WHO'S WHO AND WHAT WAS WHERE

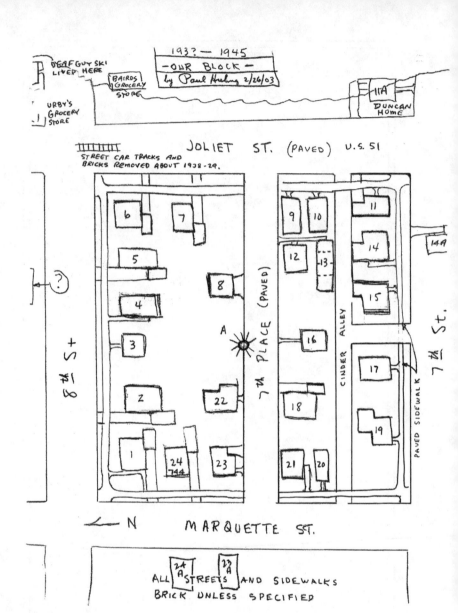

OUR BLOCK

THE MAP ON the opposite page shows the city block where I lived until I was eighteen years old. Numbers in the following list refer to numbers on the map.

1. I vaguely remember playing with Bob Simmons who lived in this corner house. (His maternal grandfather was "Pop" Munch who put pepper on his watermelon.) We were about three or four when he moved to Peru. We met again in high school to become good friends. He married Erma Domki, another classmate.

The Willoughby family moved in next. Mr. Willoughby ran a jewelry store located on the corner of Second and Marquette Streets in the Hotel Kaskaskia. Bill and Bob were the sons. Bob was closer to brother Don's age. Bill was older and became an Episcopal minister and lived in El Paso, Illinois. Bob loved airplanes and built model after model. He had so many that he would have a cleanup day, which consisted of soaking a rag in something flammable, winding up the propeller, lighting the rag, setting the plane loose, and watching it go down in flames.

The Seaton family moved in next. Tom played cornet until he got a trumpet and always won the bugle contest at Boy Scout Troup 21 outings. Anne and I were in the same grade and became close friends. She had a great sense of humor. She went off to college. While there, a friend knew a young man who had lost his wife and thought Anne

Thomas Seaton

Anne Seaton

looked like a picture the man had of his deceased wife. A blind date was arranged, and the young man nearly collapsed when he saw Anne, as she looked so much like his wife. It was a tough situation for Anne to be in, but later she married him!

2. Nate and Sadie Ginsburg. I remember a family who lived there before them. They had a girl my age, Mary Barbara Brewer, who was later written up in *Life* magazine as a "blooming starlet" of Hollywood. It didn't take hold.

Sadie paid Don and me in Indian-head pennies for weeks and weeks when we collected newspaper money. We gave them all to Maxwell Freudenburg who lived in house 23 on the map. Nate Ginsburg was a tailor whose shop was on Second Street between Joliet and Tonti Streets. They had no children that I know of.

3. One of La Salle's earliest houses. It was a very small four-room house. The Cusick family lived there first, I remember, and Don knew them better than I did. Later the Affelt family moved in. As there was no Mr. Affelt, Mrs. Affelt raised Eleanor and Francis (Frank) as best she could, which was rough during the Depression.

4. This two-story wooden frame house was first occupied by the Hanley family. The Hanleys had originally lived in a house that was torn down when I was still a kid. It was on the northwest corner of Eighth and Marquette. Mrs. Hanley was from a family that owned farm property. Her maiden name was Flaherty.

She inherited some of the farm, which her husband sold. Then he opened a tavern. Mr. Hanley was an alcoholic and made life hard for his wife and six children. Their three oldest children—Joe, Leo, and Margaret—took off for Detroit in the early '30s to work in the automobile factories that were paying $5.00 a day. This was big money in those days. My dad had a little run-in with Joe and Leo before they left for Detroit. Maybe this is why I remember the Hanley family so clearly.

The Affelts moved over to this house for a while. Mrs. Affelt got a job at the small confectionery next to the Peru Theater and became the owner and operator. I lost track of Frank, who was my age. I later met him while he was in his U.S. Army uniform and approached him only to be unrecognized by him. I asked him about living on Eighth Street until fifth or sixth grade, but he declared he had little memory of it. Even though we were in the same grade at school and walked there together, he had forgotten me. I think many kids who had it tough throughout the Depression sort of wiped it out of their memories.

5. Mr. and Mrs. Lyons lived here. We stayed out of their yard, which was lined with hedges. They had no children. He was the La Salle police detective. The day after the new tennis courts were finished—blacktopped and the nets had not yet been installed—Bill McClary and I discovered them as we were roller-skating up at Hegeler Park. Of course we

Bill McClary

skated on the courts. It was great fun until Mr. Lyons arrived with two police officers and claimed we were under arrest for skating on the tennis courts! Rev. McClary, Bill's dad, took care of that situation quite fast; in fact he recommended Bill and I go back and skate some more, but we didn't want to face the wrath of Mr. Lyons. Mr. Lyons could scare kids, but he couldn't locate any gambling in La Salle. Of course, he never asked me if I knew.

6. The Glenn family. Mr. Glenn was a brick mason and helped build the sewer system under Joliet Street when the bricks were removed and it was paved. The bricks were free to anyone who wanted to pick them up and lug them home. We three Huling boys lugged a lot home. Our dad edged flower beds with them. The Glenn family lived in the basement of their house, thereby preserving the upper floor for special occasions, I presume. There were three generations living there some of the time. A daughter, Loretta, who was a year or two behind me in school, and her younger brother sometimes resided at the corner of Eighth and Joliet.

Talking about Joliet Street: a streetcar used to run up the center of this street all the way to Eleventh, where it turned around on a turntable and came back down. We would take thin copper telephone wire, form our names, and then lay it on the tracks to be flattened and welded tight by the streetcar.

7. A very sweet couple who was older and very quiet. I don't know if they had children, but they were nice to us kids and paperboys.

8. A garage for parking two cars. Mr. Warren owned the garage. He had owned most of the entire city block at one time, and it was he who paved Seventh Place in order to utilize the space to build more houses. At one time, I was told, houses 3 and 4 operated an orchard on the sides of a gully that was behind their houses. Mr. Warren bought the land and filled it in to build houses 16, 18, and 22 and the garage used by 16 and 22. For many years a 1927 Whippet sat alongside the garage. It was great to hide behind when playing games in Seventh Place. Our dad, Thurman, made a pipe play bar and erected it on the north side of the alley near the Schemerhorn house (22). It consisted of two pipes stuck in the ground with another pipe about six feet long suspended from each vertical pipe with metal brackets he had made at the Alpha Cement Company where he worked. Don was able to sit on the pipe, throw himself backward, and land on his feet.

9. The Snow family. Bob Snow was a year younger than me. He was a good athlete and a strong Baptist. When I gave up the paper route brother Don had passed on to me, I recommended my substitute Bob receive it, and he got it.

10. The lady here was a bit strange. Not only did she appear at the door in her nightie, she had visitors from time to time. For a while we kids in the neighborhood would visit her babysitter in the evenings, but we never saw any baby. I was told the baby was a little boy three or four years old, but I never saw him. Maxwell Freudenburg said Ms. Bradbury had a boyfriend who was a local married professional, and Max knew the baby-sitter.

11A. The large house on the northeast corner of Seventh and Joliet Streets was owned by Stewart Duncan. I once threw a newspaper through the front window and then went right up to Mr. Duncan and offered to replace it. The story is detailed in "Route 11—A Good Route to Take" (page 93).

11. The Schulte family lived here until the Timm family moved in. Jane, Bill, and Bob Schulte grew up with parents who were deaf mutes. Mr. Schulte worked at the M & H Zinc Company. Mrs. Schulte gassed herself in the kitchen stove. This devastated the family. They then moved to a house near Lincoln School where Jane and an aunt were teachers,

Billy, Jane, and Bob Schulte

as I remember. Bill Schulte married a classmate of mine, Mary Urbanowski, who lived on North Gooding Street. At my fiftieth high-school class reunion, Bill took me aside and told me my dad had given him his first ride in an automobile and took him fishing for the first time, when he caught his first fish—a carp "as big as a whale."

12. The Jorgensons were nice and quiet—no children. Old Mrs. Jorgenson couldn't speak much English, but remained productive in her son's home by weaving braided rugs. My mother, Agnes, saved wool for years, cut it into strips, sewed it into a tubular shape, and then gave it to the elder Mrs. Jorgenson. For years, until my mother died, that rug graced her dining rooms wherever she lived. The rug, made in the late 1930s, is still in service, now in my son Paul's living room in Cleveland.

13. Another garage. Houses 9, 10, 12, 16, and 17 used it, as they had no other space for a garage.

14A. A house on the south side of Seventh Street where a boy lived with his mom and stepdad. He was about Don's age. The house was built on the side of a slight hill, and the boys that built model airplanes would fly them from the front porch.

14. This is where Dr. Moran lived before he was found in the Illinois River. I was told he was forced to stand in a bucket of wet cement until it hardened, then they drove his car to the river and dumped him in. The local police never investigated this case of "suicide" much. Dr. Moran, it was said, had treated some Chicago/Peoria gang members during the Prohibition era of shoot-'em-up gangs. Until the Cosgrove family moved in, we used to stay clear of that house.

The Cosgroves had three boys: Jack, who was three days younger than me; Bob, a year younger; and Jerry, younger still. We played together and grew up close friends. Seventh Street soon became our baseball, football, and sledding field. As there was no salt in those days, the slope from Joliet to Marquette Streets made for great sledding when cars packed it into ice. We also had temperature inversions that caused rain to freeze, and a few times we skated on Seventh Street and all over town.

15. This house was built by Emery and Marie Phillips, who had no children. Emery ran a Skelly filling station on Second and Gooding Streets. They built a little brick house up on Kilmer and Lafayette, across the street from Don and Lindy's house on Bucklin. The Klines, who ran a grocery store, had a son, Herbie, who was a few years younger than me. They didn't live there very long before the Bittner family with children Jack and Irene moved in. Jack was Don's age, and Irene was my age.

One night Jack was driving his father's Hudson, and brother Don was driving Dad's Model A Ford sedan, and

Jack Bittner

Irene Bittner

they got to racing around our block, ducking into alleys, etc. Don had the upper hand with the Model A because it could turn around on a dime, while Jack would have to put the Hudson in reverse to make a U-turn. Then Don had this very clever idea involving Timms' house (11), where Bob and Bill Timm, both older, resided. (Mr. Timm worked as an electrical engineer for Alpha Cement, the same place our dad worked as plant engineer.)

Don said to me, "Look! Timms' garage door is open, and there is no car inside! Next time we come around, I'll pull into the garage, and you jump out and shut the door! Jack will never know where we went!"

Great idea! So we had to open the gap between Jack's Hudson and our Model A. Everything was right on plan until Don came wheeling into the alley parallel to Timms' driveway. Don barreled down the driveway only to find Mr. Timm standing with his hands above his head reaching for the garage door . . . and his car parked inside! Our Model A was going too fast to stop, so Don wheeled to the left, through the hedge alongside the drive, across the yard, down the curb, and back to the street. Next day Mr. Timm told my dad his son had a very clever trick planned . . . if it had worked.

Irene developed early and was dating high-school boys who drove before we were out of grade school. She said good-bye to so many older fellows as they went to serve during World War II that she finally quit dating older guys and settled on one her own age. Then she said good-bye to us, too. She finally married a professional football player our same age: Gorgel was his name. I never knew what happened to Jack Bittner. Irene had twin girls and later divorced the football player.

16. This house in the alley was rented over and over again, usually to young couples. The only name I remember is Mr. McDermitt, and the reason I remember that name is because Mr. McDermitt was a crabby old man who parked his big fat car right in front of his house on Seventh Place. This blocked the gathering area for kids to play under the streetlight (marked A on the map), and he didn't want us playing around his car. One day Paul Clark, who at that time lived next-door in house 18, let air out of the tires of Mr. McDermitt's car. The wrath of the gods descended on poor Paul, but Mr. McDermitt moved away shortly thereafter.

17. Where the Christopher family lived. Mr. Christopher was a barber, and Mrs. Christopher was a golfer. They had two boys who were both older than us. The younger son, Martin, became a priest at St. Bede College west of Peru. He eventually wound up in Washington, D.C.

18. This house rented to families named Applegate, Clark, and Assalley during my growing-up years. The Applegates had a baby daughter named Ardin, and that name has stuck with me all these years. I know nothing more about them. Next, the Clarks moved from 22 to 18 with two kids: Ed, older than me, and Paul, just my age, who became a long-time friend. After the Clarks came Frank Assalley with one boy, also named Frank, younger than the rest of us. Frank senior operated a Packard garage at First and Tonti Streets. After the Assalleys came the Hendersons with older kids. I was getting older, too, so we never associated much.

19. A great house for girls to move into. I never remember any boys living there, only girls, and they didn't seem to stay very long in that house. A classmate of Don's, Margery Feurer, lived there. They were in seventh grade together at Lincoln School. One family named Scheinzer had three lovely girls my age and younger and a mother who made sure the girls stayed close to home under her watchful eye. There was really no reason for the mother to fear. All the kids in the neighborhood had fun together as a family would. To have a crush on one of the neighbor girls was like kissing a sister. Should an attraction show up, as it did from time to time, the romance quickly cooled with no loss in friendship. Anyway, because of the cautious Mrs. Scheinzer, we generally played in the large yard on the Marquette Street side. The names I remember are Becky, Patty, and Vickie Scheinzer.

Later on the granddaughter of the original Mr. Warren, who had owned most of the city block, moved into this house. Her name was Norma.

20. A family named Dooley lived here. Their phone number was 1546R. I know that because we were on the same party line and our phone number was 1546W. They had twin little girls who always played nuns. I wonder if that is what they are now.

21. This one is difficult for me to remember. I think during the depths of the Depression a Mrs. Murphy baked bread in the basement and sold it to make money. Later a Cassidy family moved in with older kids. Ed Cassidy was in Don's high-school class and played football on L-P's (La Salle-Peru High School's) winning team. Then the

Edward Cassidy

Tinny Cosgrove

Golden family moved in, and eventually Jean Golden married Tinny Cosgrove, a local gambler and nightclub owner. Jean was about a year older than me. "Pop" Golden was active in Boy Scouting.

22. This place housed quite a few families before the Schemerhorn family with Allen, a year or two older than me, and Sally Ann, many years younger. The first I remember was the young Clark family I already mentioned in 18. Before 22 they had lived temporarily in 23 with Tom Clark, an old bachelor, and two unmarried schoolteachers. One aunt taught at Washington Grade School, and the other aunt worked in the high-school library.

After the Clarks came the Mathew family with kids Annabel, oldest and older than me; Roy, older than me; and Marion, who was my age and in my class at school. Roy's dad had been in World War I, and Don remembers him telling Don to take out ten thousand dollars of GI insurance and keep it as long as he could. Don has a paid-up policy, thanks to this good advice. Many years later, about 1965, I met Roy working in the tool room at the Caterpillar plant in Joliet. It was good to see him again and talk about Seventh Place.

Marion Mathew

23. When the Clarks left this house, the Freudenburgs moved in. Mrs. Freudenburg was one of my favorite people

Tinny's Silver Congo

because we had a date every Tuesday night at eight to listen to Fibber McGee and Molly. She was a master at tinting photographs taken by Mr. Freudenburg before the days of color film. Mr. Freudenburg was a fine photographer and had a studio on the second floor above the building next to Jensen's Jewelry Store. Marcella was a little older than Don, and Maxwell was brother John's age. Mr. Freudenburg kept dabbling in other projects. Once they moved out to a farm where he tried to raise chickens. Another scheme was to raise chinchillas in their basement. That didn't work out. Another adventure was frying cheese chips in hot oil and selling them from the five-and-ten-cent store. They tasted delicious, but he dropped that endeavor. The alfalfa vitamin scheme also failed. He always went back to photography. Don has an excellent picture of the La Salle Congregational Church choir members that Mr. Freudenburg took on Easter Sunday 1938

Maxwell Freudenburg driving a Maxwell.

(see page 74). I'm in the second row behind Joan Gebhardt, Lindy is the last girl in row one, and Don is holding the flag in back of Lindy.

The Freudenburgs' son Maxwell went on to become a lawyer and lived in Washington, D.C. He married, had a son, and divorced, and he and his son now live in Durango, Colorado. Marcella married a coal mine inspector and lives in Pineville, Kentucky.

23A. Mr. Archie was the Ford dealer at Third and Bucklin where I worked when it was a Pontiac dealership. The Archies moved to Des Moines where son David, who was John's age, became publisher of a magazine. David died a few years ago. We had planned to lunch together when I was in Des Moines, but we never made it.

The Harls lived in this house after the Archies moved. Eljean (short for Ella-Jean, but I think Eljean was her real name) was a classmate of mine in grade school till about grade five. Her older brother was Sidney. They moved to Spring Valley. I lost track of the Harls until a choral concert at L-P where Pop Sellew featured Sidney as a guest singer from Hall High School. Later, when I was in JC (junior college), Eljean showed up, and we renewed our acquaintance. Eljean was our choral piano accompanist while I was in junior college.

Don "Pop" Sellew

One day a few of us from JC went to Spring Valley to drink coffee, and Eljean told me it was her mother who hit John (see "Brother John's Accident" on page 209). She told me that our folks had called Mrs. Harl immediately upon returning from the hospital to assure the Harls that there would be no lawsuit from the Hulings. This had impressed the Harls for years, and Eljean's mother had asked Eljean to remind me of how great my parents were.

Eljean had a boyfriend while we were in JC. We teased her about not telling us who it was she was seeing. It turned out to be Pop Sellew, that dirty old man! Eljean would be his third wife—quite a scandal at the time.

24. The last house on the list is where I grew up with Alice, Don, and John. Alice, eight years my senior, never played much in the neighborhood, but Don, John, and I wore out the sidewalks and play areas. And, as you can see, I think I knew about everything that went on in our block.

❊ ❊ ❊

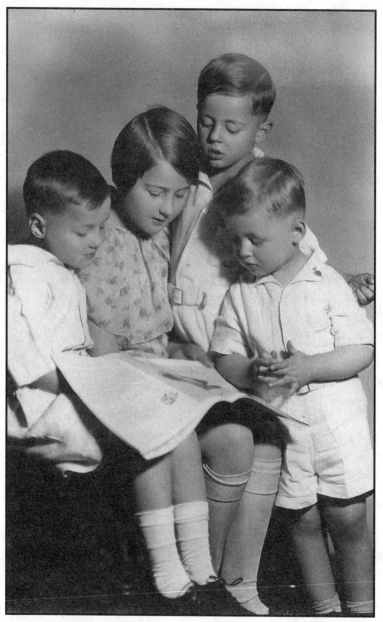

Huling kids: Alice, 11; Don, 7; John, 5; Paul, 4

Brother John's Accident

ONE EVENING AFTER supper, we were playing hide-and-go-seek in the Willoughby front yard. John ran across Marquette Street and hid behind a parked car. When he thought it was safe to run across the street and touch base to be free, he darted out right in front of a Model T car that hit him and knocked him down.

The driver, Mrs. Harl, picked him up and took him directly to St. Mary's Hospital. Don ran to the house and told Mom and Dad that John had been hit by a car. They immediately backed out the Model A Ford and drove up to the hospital. John was passing blood in his urine, so Dr. Burke knew his kidney had been damaged. It seemed to heal up OK, but in later years, when he had open-heart surgery, it was his kidney that failed, and he died.

My Grandfather, John Huling
(December 28, 1858–April 13, 1947)

MY GRANDFATHER, JOHN Huling, was born in Carysville, Ohio, on December 28, 1858. He was the second child of nine. There were seven girls. The youngest child was a boy, Uncle Charlie. John didn't have a middle name, so he gave himself one—Henry—I think when he got married. The log cabin in which Grandpa was born was still standing in 1991.

John's father and mother, James and Mary, were given land by Mary's father (Bowersock), who bought the land from the person who had homesteaded the land. Homesteading meant you owned the land if you lived on it for five years, once you received permission to do so from the U.S.

government. The homesteader sold shortly after receiving the clear title. He lived in a log cabin, now gone, that was near a flowing spring. It appeared from the contour of the land that the homesteader had a cellar under his cabin. Although this could have been for protection from Indians, it is more likely that it was needed to house animals in winter or to store food supplies to make it through winter. The homesteader was not a farmer; he only cleared enough land to exist until he could gain title and sell.

John's father, James, ran a millrace sawmill. It was located beside the creek behind the log cabin on Taylor's property. James cleared land and sold the timber as boards. After cutting a tree, using a six-foot two-man saw, the logs were hauled, dragged, or floated to the saw. Once mounted on a carriage and anchored, the log and carriage (which was on rails, and the rails on an incline) would gravity-feed into the saw blade. The blade was powered by water flowing from the dammed-up creek through a waterway to the waterwheel, which turned the saw blade. The saw blade rotated slowly. James would start a cut before breakfast, eat, milk the cows, and maybe one board would be cut. Then he'd start another cut before cutting another tree, bury a stump, etc. etc.

The land James cleared became the farm for John. Of course, there were stumps and huge stones to be buried or hauled away first.

John worked with horses. He never owned a tractor. The horses pulled one eight-inch plow, a six-foot disk, an eight-foot harrow, a two-row corn planter, a wheat and oats planter, a one-row cultivator plow, a side-bar mower, a hay rake (rear-lift), a binder, a hay wagon that converted to a grain wagon, and a flat bed (boards on which stones and stumps could be rolled). That was it except for a couple of hay elevators that

Hulings, 1886
FRONT ROW: **Nora, Charles Adolphus;** MIDDLE ROW: **Margaret, James Milton, Mary Jane Bowersock, Mary Jane Huling;** BACK ROW: **Orpha, Sarah Ann, John Henry, Clare, Laura. All of James Milton Huling's children, with the exception of Charles, were born in a one-room log cabin, 1856-1875.**

broke down too quickly on rough land and were placed behind the barn to rot.

The few times John had used three horses as a team was when it came time to pull the combine. Otherwise, he only used two and did not overwork them. He was gentle with his animals. In his youth, he had a team of three mules, which my grandmother told me would work harder for John than any team in the area. Of course, John was on the other end of this hardworking team. By the time I knew him, he was working two horses gently.

There was one other machine involved with the farm—a thrashing machine. George Bailey from Carysville ran the thrasher. That's all he did as far as I knew. When I asked Grandpa, he agreed. It was George's job to make sure the thrasher worked, without failure, from the middle of June through the end of July when wheat, then oats were ready to harvest. About twenty farmers owned the thrasher as a co-op. It was powered by a huge steam engine. It was old, and so was George, when I was a boy. George was very serious about his job, although he was so fat and out of shape from ten months of reconditioning the thrasher, he had trouble getting up and down. George didn't farm. He predicted weather from his front porch. If I didn't want to be asked a lot of questions on my way to the Carysville store, I rode my bike the back road. This had been downtown before the train tracks went in a mile from Carysville, at Rosewood.

Downtown Carysville was where my grandmother lived

Don sitting on Grandpa Huling's lap with father Thurman and Grandma Sarah Virginia, "Jenny," 1929.

as a girl. Her father ran the Inn. That's where my father was born. Sarah Virginia (Jenny, as she was better known), my grandmother, knew all about everybody somehow. Anyway, her father also dug wells in the area. One year, all the wells in Carysville went dry but one. The woman who owned the well wouldn't give my great-grandfather water because he was a Democrat (or whatever). So he dug a new well at the corner of Main and the "heart of town." By then this woman's well had run dry, and she was afraid to go ask for water. "I don't care what you are, you can have water," she was told. (My dad, Thurman, told this story.)

My great-grandfather, James Milton Huling, died in 1898, which left his wife, Mary, and John to carry on. John was forty, married, and the father of a ten-year-old son, Thurman, my dad. John's younger brother, Charles, was eighteen years younger than John and wasn't much help with heavy farm work. Charlie had a hernia that was thought to be somewhat rare as the times for it to cause Charlie pain seemed to come before heavy work.

At least four of John's seven sisters still lived at home and would remain dependent on their mother and John to provide for them until about 1920. The girls were well-educated for the day, attending schools as far away as Cincinnati. Four married so late in life they couldn't have children, and one married so late she could only have one child. John's mother, Mary, managed the farm finances until she died.

Around the turn of the century, the farm raised cattle, pigs, chickens, geese, and horses. The women canned, gardened, milked the cow, and did many household chores. Sometimes the women had to help in the fields at harvesttime. Everyone pitched in.

The one thing John would not do was kill an animal or fowl he had raised. He would leave the farm and return when he knew the deed had been done.

John had four years of school as a boy. He could only go to school in winter. He carried a hot potato to school each day to keep himself warm and then ate it for lunch. Potatoes were always his favorite food.

By the time John was fourteen, he no longer went to school. But he was the addition champion of the area. Seems they would have get-togethers at the school where there would be contests to see who could add up columns of numbers the fastest, and John would add them up as they wrote them down and had the answer by the time the last number was dictated. So they changed the rules and wrote the numbers on the blackboard first and then covered them until they were ready for the contest. He still won.

When I was a boy and Grandpa was in his eighties, he would ask me what day of the month it was. Then he would ask me to add up the numbers above and below that day (for example, all Wednesdays of the month) and tell him the answer. Now Grandpa couldn't see the calendar from his rocking chair, but he would tell me the answer before I could tell him. I would try to trick him by telling him it was, let's say, Thursday, February 11, or find a thirty-one day month with five Mondays, etc. He knew all the tricks. Then he'd say that maybe the schools aren't as good as they used to be when he was a boy.

Mary, John's mother, died in 1920. John was sixty-two. He inherited one-ninth of the farm. The farm was broken into four pieces; two acres at the corner of Route 29 went to John's sister Mary Jane, known as Aunt Jennie Williams. She made it into a religious campground.

The other approximately eighty acres on that side of the road were sold to Oscar and Ora Burkhold. This land had the large house built by James and the log cabin. It also has a barn that the year after it was built was turned 90 degrees on its foundation by a tornado. The barn still stands as turned, on the Kurt Taylor property. All the land remaining was divided so that Uncle Charlie got the flat land near Carysville and John got more land, but less tillable. The boys didn't exactly "get" the land—they bought it from their sisters. One sister (Mary Jane) wanted more for her share than the others,

Log cabin where all the Huling family children, except Charles, were born and raised. Vicklye with her father Don, 1960.

and one (Nora) accepted nothing from John for her share in thanks for all John had done for her.

John had wanted to go to California before he was married, but the gold rush stories that got back to Carysville were not as glowing as they had been when he was a boy. That is the only mention he ever made to me of ever dreaming of leaving the area.

John did travel to Columbus to settle the deed to the farm. He couldn't afford the train, or didn't want to take it. Anyway, he hitched a wagon and on his way through Carysville picked up a friend who had never traveled further from home than St. Paris (seven miles). After the first day out, John's friend wanted to know how far they had traveled. John told him they had reached Urbana. "I never dreamed the world was this big!" said John's friend. The year would have been 1921.

Another time John left the farm by train to go to Fort Wayne, Indiana, to be "dried out." Alcohol had caused John to nearly lose the farm. Thereafter, John was sober except the day in 1943 when my sister, Alice, got married. He was retrieved from Uncle Charlie's in a wheelbarrow. That was the day I learned of Grandpa's past problems.

Another friend of John's lived on the farm. He was a native Indian who was raised on the farm. He camped in the woods near the spring. He could stay as long as he wanted. My dad knew him, too, and showed me where the Indian had lived. The pond now covers the area or has altered it so much I can't exactly point the area out anymore. The Indian would work sometimes when he wanted to, but the Hulings had always told him he could plant gardens and hunt and live there as long as he wished. One day he packed up and said he was going to California. I think he made it.

John had cattle all his life. He raised cattle from his herd of about twenty to twenty-five head. He would keep what he considered the best to milk. He sold those he didn't think had the coloring or shape he wanted to keep. In other words, he had his own strain after sixty-plus years of breeding. He was never around when the trailer came to pick one up and take it to market.

As a boy I used to go to cattle auctions with Wilbur Hart, the hired man on the farm. When a bull of John's went on the block, there were many puzzled faces amongst the bidders. John's bulls had square rumps, full bodies, and long legs. They were very alert and active. No breed name could be attached. They usually bid quite high compared to others on the block. Sometimes when he auctioned young heifers, someone would sort of mention under his breath to me that Grandpa's cows didn't give much milk. I would act surprised to hear that. However, the quantity of milk a cow produced didn't seem to be one of John's criteria. In fact, Grandmother always said if they gave milk, John got rid of them.

When John walked the farm, he usually had friends with him. Cats ran under his feet, chickens hustled, cows fell in line, and horses trotted around. They were all his friends,

Three Generations of Huling Men
Paul, Don, Grandfather John, Thurman, and John, 1947.

and he didn't fuss over them, they fussed over him. When a bull got too aggressive with John, it was time to sell him. Three times when John was in his eighties, different bulls challenged him. Once he was fixing fence when one got overly friendly; John had to use the hammer to convince that bull. Another bull pinned him up against the barn, and John managed to slip out of his bib overalls. Finally, one got him down and would have overcome him had not Wilbur arrived with a pitchfork. John said he would have been all right as long as the bull kept him in the mud. After that, all bulls but one were sold while they were calves.

When John was eighty-four, he still insisted on driving the binder, because he knew he could handle two horses to pull it. Normally three horses are used, but Gramp would run the fields so the horses didn't have to pull the binder up the steep hills under full load. It was while going up a steep hill that the binder wheel hit a rock and threw Gramp forward off the binder, just behind the horses. As he flew through the air, he gently hollered, "Whoa," and the horses seemed to freeze.

John never pulled on the reins to stop a horse once he had trained them to obey commands. At eighty-four he proved this to be a good practice.

I believe it was after the clover-Patterson incident that Grandmother (Jenny) took over the finances and the budgeting of the farm. There were some years when the price of corn was so low they burned it instead of coal to heat the stove. One Depression year, Dad refinanced our house in Illinois to help make payments on the farm. This was not a get-rich-quick farm, but the folks always had enough food and considered themselves well-off for the times.

One day when we returned to the farm from a trip to St. Paris, I found Grandmother in the kitchen crying. She was holding a folder of paper and hid it under the kitchen towels in the cupboard drawer. I asked what was wrong, and she asked me not to reveal to anyone why she was crying. That day she had made the last payment on the farm. It now belonged to them. Together, they had worked about fifty-five years. Should she tell Grandpa? He was eighty-five. He didn't know she had made the last payment. She didn't want me to tell him. She couldn't get herself to tell him. She would, later—after she wept.

John was a quiet person those years that I knew him. He was always pleasant, never demanding or loud. When I think of all the people whose lives he affected because he worked so faithfully and so long, it's no wonder I want to admire and remember him.

Mom

MOM WAS BORN in Kansas in 1895. Her father was a railroad engineer who had migrated to Kansas from upper New York. Mom's mother was a dyed-in-the-wool Kansan.

During her early years, Mom learned to play the piano. She played well enough that, with her father as chaperon, she played piano for Saturday matinee silent movies. A lot of what she played was ragtime of that era. She learned pipe organ at a large Presbyterian church in her town of Fort Scott. After high school, she taught in a totally integrated grade school until my dad spotted her. Dad was from Ohio, working in Kansas. Not long afterward, they moved to Illinois and raised their family.

Tragedy struck when the flu epidemic took their first-born daughter at age fourteen months. Determination kept Mom going. In fact, determination best describes my mom. If ever there was a woman who would see things through, it was Mom. The day before she died, her minister visited her in the hospital, and she assured him she was up-to-date on her Bible study class assignment and had not fallen behind.

The Great Depression found Mom with four young children and Dad's salary cut in half. She sewed white shirts for Dad, dresses for sister Alice, and outfits for brothers Don, John, and me. We three boys were born within a three-year period, so my brothers passed outgrown things on to me. Because my mom made the clothes, I was never ashamed of that. She had her hands full but still found time to garden, do laundry, iron, practice piano, and sing. She encouraged her children to sing, too.

Each of her children practiced daily on instruments. Alice, on piano, majored in music in college. Don still performs in orchestras on violin. John excelled on cello all his life until he died. I was somewhat different, so I switched from flute to tuba, washboard, and song. I quit my day job to become a "wasboarditionist." Mom loved my wife's and my ragtime duo.

Agnes Hawthorne Huling

Thurman Huling

Mom also loved to garden. She had beautiful flower beds around our small lot and joined the Garden Club when her boys were grown enough to look after themselves. Recognized as an organizer, she soon became chairperson. The local Women's Club also sought her leadership, so she later became chair of the Women's Club.

But Mom gave up leadership roles for a munitions plant because she could help with the war effort. With two sons in service, her garden and her clubs would have to take a backseat. There was a war to win, and Mom was determined to get her boys back home again as soon as possible.

Mom and Dad retired to Ohio, to the family farm, where Mom updated the house, grew huge flower gardens, and took a regular pipe organist position at a large church in Sidney. Although her family was raised, she took in Dad's aunt and uncle, who needed help, and cared for them at her home till the end of their lives.

Yes, Mom was determined. When her eyesight failed and she could no longer see music, or the keys on the piano, she learned to play by ear. When Dad died and she was alone on the farm and blind, she kept going with all the financial details in her head. With household help, she stuck it out until she recognized the end was near. But she never fell behind on her Bible studies. How did she do that? Determination, and her love of God.

Once I tried to write a poem for my mom for Mother's Day, but it didn't turn out the way I intended. She called it "different." Later I entered the poem in a contest, and it was published. Mom would have liked that. She always encouraged me to be me, even if I was . . . different. I love her for that.

My Aunt Nora Huling Baker
by Don Huling

THE FIRST TIME I visited Columbus, Ohio, I was four years old. The year was 1928. My dad, Thurman, had been called back to New York to testify in a lawsuit his company, the Alpha Cement Company, had against one of its suppliers of equipment that was not performing properly. My mom, Agnes, was left at home in La Salle with Alice, John, and Paul while I came to Ohio to be taken care of by my great-aunt Nora Baker. All I remember of Columbus was a bright sunny morning as Dad and I got off the train and walked outside the depot to be picked up by our Ohio relatives.

Aunt Nora and Uncle John Baker's farm was on Route 36 (now Ohio Route 235), about a mile west of the road that led to Carysville and Grandma and Grandpa Huling's farm. The Bakers had a young man living with them, Wallace Voorhese, who helped out on the farm and also went to St.

STANDING: **Laura Huling Ashmore, Nora Huling Baker, Charles A. Huling, Thurman;** SITTING: **Paul, Don, and John.**

Paris High School. Aunt Nora and Uncle John had married late in life and had no children of their own. They made a home for Wallace, who was an orphan and had lived in the orphanage just south of Sidney. Wallace had black hair that he combed straight back, and he could play the piano. Aunt Nora had taught piano when she was younger. She and her sister Maggie had graduated from the Cincinnati Conservatory of Music and had returned to Champaign and Shelby Counties to teach children in their homes. They each drove a horse and buggy.

Uncle John Baker had a big black horse named Frank. The horse was so big and I was so small that I was afraid of him. I remember yelling "Here come Frank. Here come Frank" to try to scare Aunt Nora. She would go along with me and pretend to be frightened, and then I'd laugh.

One day Uncle John brought home a rabbit for Aunt Nora to cook for supper. He didn't shoot the rabbit—he killed it by throwing a wrench at it. He had been cutting a field of wheat. As he went around and around the field, the standing wheat that was left in the middle got smaller and smaller. This is where all the game came to hide. As the last of the standing wheat was cut, the animals would run in all directions. Uncle John was ready and, as they say, "brought home the bacon."

Aunt Nora performed a lot of tasks around the house. One was ironing on Tuesday. Monday was washday, but on Tuesday she would get a fire going in the kitchen stove, set the steel irons on the top, then take them off, one at a time, and iron clothes until the iron cooled off. She only had one handle that she would use to lift the hot iron. She'd iron the clothes, then set the cooled iron back on the stove. Lindy and I still have one of these irons that Aunt Nora used so many years ago.

Making cream toffee and ice cream were two jobs I watched with watering mouth. Aunt Nora used pure cream for both of these delicious rich cream products. There was a big iron hook on the wall of her kitchen she used to pull the cream taffy until it turned stiff. That first bite was delicious! And the ice cream—a quart jar of canned strawberries usually went into the ice-cream freezer with all the other ingredients. I was too little to turn the handle that made the mixers move inside the freezer, but when it came time to eat the final product, I was first in line!

The Bakers took animals they had raised to the meat-packing plant over in Pique, Ohio. They would return with hot dogs and baloney—plus cash for the bank, of course. I remember getting quite sick from eating too many hot dogs. Aunt Nora called her sister Laura Ashmore from Sidney for advice. I threw up and was fine, but went a lot slower on the hot dogs after that.

They had a party line telephone back in 1928. One day Aunt Nora was expecting a phone call from one of her sisters who lived in Sidney, but had to go outside and hang up the laundry. She said, "Donny, you stay right here by the phone. If it rings, you get up on this chair and answer it. If it's for me, tell them to wait a minute and let the receiver hang straight down, then come and get me." I still remember lying on the floor in the warm sun waiting for the phone to ring. It never did, but Aunt Nora gave me a big hug and kiss for helping out, anyway.

Uncle John and Aunt Nora sold their farm there on Route 36 in 1938 and moved to a farm nearer Sidney. There was a woods on part of this farm down by the swimming hole. Aunt Nora had a big garden where she raised sweet corn, green beans, and lots of strawberries. There were chickens, horses, cows, and pigs that all had to be taken care of. Nora and John needed more help, so they got another young man from the orphanage in Sidney. His name was Cappy, and he was a real hard worker.

Uncle John died from cancer the next summer, so Aunt Nora was really dependent on her two boys. I spent two summers on this farm helping out wherever I could. The most fun was going to Sidney on Saturday nights, swimming in the swimming hole down at the creek, and visiting neighbors in the evening. My brother John stayed with my grandparents, and I remember riding the bicycle Aunt Nora bought for me over to see John, as I was homesick and getting tired of being away from La Salle every summer.

Aunt Nora eventually moved off the farm into a nice bungalow on Brooklyn Avenue in Sidney. The house had been her oldest sister Sally's house, and I remember taking produce from Aunt Nora's garden into Sidney on Saturday night to give to Aunt Sally. Nora was quite close to her other sister, Laura Ashmore. Both sisters were widows by the

Aunt Nora in Cincinnati

middle of the '30s, when I was still spending my summers on the farm. Aunt Laura lived down the street from Aunt Sally.

Wallace and Cappy found jobs in Sidney, married, and had families of their own. Aunt Nora kept in touch with "her boys," as she called them, and they would visit her as her last days approached. She had a housekeeper who lived with her at this time. The year was 1941, and I had graduated from high school. Nora didn't trust the housekeeper completely and was desirous to see some of her possessions that weren't in the bank or in real estate get into the hands of those she had enjoyed earlier in life.

One day, back in La Salle, my mother Agnes received a letter from Aunt Nora, mailed with only a three-cent stamp on it. The letter was not registered or special delivery or anything at all that would have been appropriate for what was inside—only a first-class, three-cent stamp. Well, my mother was flabbergasted when she opened the letter and out came seven diamonds, each wrapped in tissue paper. Aunt Nora had "smuggled" them out of the house, so to speak, as she didn't trust the housekeeper. Her instructions were to have the diamonds made into a ring for Donny, as she still called me, for his high-school graduation present.

We took the diamonds down to Jensen Jewelers. Mr. Jensen, a fine jeweler, came up with two designs. The first would have placed the three small diamonds on each side of the large center stone parallel to the ring finger, which would have made a rather massive ring. The second design, which we chose without much hesitation, placed the small stones on either side of the large center diamond in descending size. The stones had been in a necklace Aunt Nora wore as a young woman and will remain in this setting as long as the ring remains in our family. On the inside of the ring band are engraved the following initials: NHB (Nora Huling Baker), DJH (Donald James Huling).

The last time I saw Aunt Nora was in the fall of 1948. Our daughter Donalyn was just a few months old, and we were on our way from Berwick, where Donalyn had been born on July 3, to La Salle prior to having our little house trailer moved to Huntington, West Virginia. Aunt Nora was on her deathbed, but although she was almost blind, she recognized who we were. She took my left hand, felt the diamond ring carefully, smiled, then asked about our baby. Lindy placed Donalyn in her arms, and again a big smile came over her face. "But you should have stockings for this child," she said as she felt Donalyn's little legs. She was thinking of others right up to the end of her life.

My Sister Alice

ALICE WAS EIGHT years old before I was born. Alice was followed by Don, John, and me, Paul. She was preceded by Mary Virginia, who died during the Spanish influenza epidemic of 1918 at the age of fourteen months, a year before Alice was born.

There is no way for me to express the loss of Mary Virginia to my mother and father, because they never talked about her or the terrible times they had during the epidemic. What I learned from family history is that Mary, Mom, and Dad all came down with influenza while living in Chanute, Kansas. Mary's body was shipped to Ohio for burial. Mom and Dad were too ill to attend the funeral. I write about Mary because Alice told me, when she was in her twenties, how she suffered, not from lack of love from our parents, but because she had felt, all her life, that she had to make up for the loss of Mary to our parents.

Alice and Don, 1924

She felt she had not been capable of doing that. I am sure Mary's death affected Alice much more than it affected her three younger brothers.

Alice was an extremely good student, a tough act for her siblings to follow. She was not an outgoing person until her later years of high school, and there it was guarded. I remember when she played the lead character in a play taken from the Booth Tarkington book *Seventeen*. She was the hit of the show as she played the ukulele and sang to the leading man. I don't know when Alice decided to major in music, but her action in that play displayed a talent I had never seen before. Alice taught me the words to songs that were popular at the time, including "The Old Spinning Wheel" and "Red Sails in the Sunset."

One night, as she sat at the desk in the dining room doing her studies, she lit a cigarette! Now that was a true display of independence! Mom and Dad smelled the smoke and came running. Because of the look on Mother's face, I don't remember ever smoking in front of her, at least until I was out of the navy. I now wish I had never started!

Alice graduated from Oberlin College with a degree in music in 1941. This was the same year Don graduated from high school and I graduated from eighth grade. Mom and Dad attended her graduation. She was the first Huling to graduate from college.

It had not been easy for our parents to put Alice through college. The Great Depression had begun when Alice was ten, and the economy had not fully recovered when Alice graduated.

Alice got the job of teaching music to all the public grade schools in La Salle. This was a fortunate break for Alice as she could live at home. A car was required for the job, so

Dad walked to work while Alice drove the Model A Ford from school to school.

Just before the school year started in La Salle, Alice received a person-to-person long-distance call from Oberlin College. She was asked to return to Oberlin to teach. That was a tremendous compliment to Alice and our family. But Alice had signed on to teach locally, so she turned the job down.

After a year of teaching, Alice married Edward P. Haugen, a consulting engineer who specialized in designing conveyors and manufacturing problems associated with space allocations within existing facilities. Ed's talents were in great demand during and after the second world war. As Ed was past draft age, his contribution to the war effort was solving knotty problems involved with war production.

Alice, besides raising three children—Christie, James, and Connie—took on the task of choir director at our Congregational church. I probably would have sung tenor in the choir no matter who was directing, but it helped my attendance to choir practice that a lovely alto named Jean, my future wife, sat in front of me.

Alice continued to direct choirs and play organ for churches the rest of her life. Because Ed was eighteen years her senior and had been self-employed all his life, there was not much retirement income, so what Alice earned helped with their finances.

Alice and Ed Haugan

Ed and Alice moved from Illinois to Ohio to be near Mom and Dad. For many years, our folks were in declining health. Alice managed to look after their finances as well as help manage the farms belonging to our parents.

One major accomplishment of Alice and Ed was to harvest the stand of walnut trees that Dad had marked and followed over the years. Before Dad died in 1986, he saw the rewards of his efforts as a true farmer in the form of a check for over $40,000 as payment for those trees.

Mom died two years after Dad. Once again, it was Alice who looked after Mom even as Ed's health was failing, and so was hers. Alice died twenty-two days after Mom died. She had undergone a much postponed hip surgery the day before her death. She was sixty-nine.

Ed was devastated. "It wasn't supposed to end like this," he told me. "I was to go first." He died soon after, with Connie at his side.

There are many factors, I suppose, that influenced Alice's life, but she always remained close to me and the rest of the family. She was a good sister. I miss her.

Don continues to remember Alice:

DOCTOR EDMUND BURKE took care of the Huling clan as long as we lived in La Salle. Alice got a large splinter in her thigh that I remember Doctor removing. I almost got the end of my left-hand ring finger cut off when just a kid. Doctor sewed it back on. Barbara Burke was one of Alice's close girlfriends.

Alice returned one spring, while still in college, with Dale Heart, who had proposed to her. It didn't work out, as his parents were more attentive to Alice than he was. He was a good bridge player, however. Brother John and I just didn't know enough about the game to beat Alice and Dale. Now Ed Haugen was another kind of bridge player. He wanted to play every hand, no matter how good or poor the cards dealt to him were. Mom and Dad were very good bridge players. They enjoyed duplicate bridge. They found it hard to play with Ed.

Alice acquired Mom's electronic organ and moved it to Sidney. I have a video of Alice playing the electric organ and Mom playing the piano by ear. Mom was legally blind at this stage of her life. Both Ed and Thurman enjoyed hearing their spouses play music they knew and could relate to.

My Brother John

I REMEMBER THE day—I just don't remember exactly how old I was, but I think I was fifteen—when I discovered my brother John and I were very good friends. Before this particular autumn day, John and I tolerated each other, yet we had never been close to each other. From the day I'm recalling until, and after, John's death, we realized we were as close as brothers could be.

John and I had a lot of catching up to do, although we never talked about that. We had many good times together. John taught me a lot about life, God, family, and to drive a car.

John was approaching eighteen. This meant he faced the draft or enlistment—his choice. He chose to enlist in the Army Air Corps in hope of flying. If he could pass the physical he would be a part of World War II and be assured of his college education when he returned. He didn't pass. He thought he had slipped past the army doctor who checked heartbeats, but was called back for a further check. Then another doctor verified what the first doctor had detected. John was devastated. He wanted to defend his country more than anything.

Brother Don was already in the air force. He was the oldest, John next, then me. The spread in age for we three brothers was three years. As a kid, John was first to get measles, mumps, chickenpox, colds, and strep throat. The strep throat led to rheumatic fever that damaged his heart so badly he spent sixth grade in bed. Sometimes, like Christmas that year, John couldn't make it back to bed from the couch in the living room because there were stairs to climb. That was a very quiet Christmas as we prayed that John would regain his strength. He began taking digitalis to stimulate his heart, which seemed to improve his condition. Listening to the radio that year was his activity.

Before John's sickness, we were not very brotherly toward one another. We lacked common interests. John loved to hunt with Dad, while I hated it. John and Don had BB guns, and John could hit the bull's-eye most every time. (Mom sent the guns to our grandparent's farm to get them out of town.) John couldn't fix anything, it seemed, while I fixed everything I could find to fix. John got straight A's, even when he was down and a tutor came to our house twice a week. I was an average student not much interested in what was taught at school.

One thing John and I shared as we grew up was church. We attended Sunday school, played in the Sunday school orchestra, sang in the choirs, and joined the Boy Scouts.

John spent seventh grade on our grandparent's farm where he went to school in Rosewood, Ohio. On the farm that year, John realized his future was open spaces, not cities. He hunted, trapped, fished, helped in ways he could, and slowly became stronger. He also learned to rest when his body told him to do so and to be careful not to overdo activities or work.

John loved to fish. I didn't like the mosquitoes that seemed to love me and leave him alone. When we were small, John would take an old bamboo fishing poll from the farm barn, and we would walk to the stream to fish. (This was the stream my great-grandfather had dammed up to power his sawmill.) Somehow Isabel, the cat, would always spot us, or find us, as we fished. She ate all we caught, which were little shiners. I couldn't stand to sit and let the bugs bite, so I'd dig worms for John as he fished.

The summer John returned home to Illinois from the farm in Ohio, the doctor told him he had to rest three hours every afternoon. In order to enforce this, all three of us boys had to rest three hours every afternoon. I complained at first, but the room we shared was the room above the garage which had windows on all four sides, ten windows in all. It never got too hot with all the windows open. Once again, we listened to the radio. Before, when John was confined to bed, we listened to Lulu Belle and Scotty in the mornings and Jack Armstrong, Little Orphan Annie, and Captain Midnight in the afternoons. Now we listened to Ma Perkins and One Man's Family. We went from breakfast-food series to soap operas.

Of course, it was early to bed for us, too, so we'd listen to radio stations from the south side of Chicago, where we'd hear Dixieland jazz, boogie-woogie, and of course, music from the Aragon and Trianon Ballrooms, where the big bands played. It wasn't all bad to be confined with John.

Finally, near the end of summer that year, the doctor told John he could ride a bike. So John got an early-morning paper route to pay for the bike and make money. He got a loan from the bank for twenty-six dollars to pay for the bike. His paper route took him all over town delivering the Chicago *Tribune* and some kind of racing form. He didn't have to collect money, but he did have to deliver seven days a week. When it snowed, Don and I would help, while Dad drove our Model A Ford.

To get into shape to ride the bike, John pitched to me. I crouched in the garage below our bedroom, while John threw to me from the proper distance out in the driveway. It was good exercise for John, and he did get good at it; so good, in fact, that he pitched a perfect game. He wasn't supposed to play, but one team would have had to forfeit their game because they didn't have a pitcher, so John filled in. He never pitched another game after that, but I was proud to have been his catcher as he learned.

About the time John and I became close friends, we got a job one fall day on a farm. The job came by way of an employment agency ad in the newspaper, and it paid quit well. The job turned out to be part of the World War II effort. A large farm had planted acres and acres of hemp. Hemp has another name or two—marijuana being one, pot another. We were not told what we would be doing when we applied for the job, but were extensively interviewed individually. We were transported to the job in the back of a closed truck so we would never know where the farm was located.

Our job that day was to turn the long stems of hemp over so it would dry evenly. While doing so, with John as my work master, a piece of a leaf got in my eye. It was terribly painful. John lay me down out of the wind and with a corner of his handkerchief removed the leaf—now broken into many pieces—from my eye. I was impressed with his skill and gentleness, but more than that was the confidence and trust I felt in his hands.

John soon left home to study forestry at Iowa State, and a year later I joined the navy. I boxed up all my clothes, shoes, and coats and sent them to John, as he had no money to buy clothes. He wrote me back a big-brother letter with advice: take naps, but don't wear anything tight; when wearing a white shirt, wear a tie; when being interviewed for a job, ask yourself if you would want the interviewer to work for you

John's Clark Gable smile

and assume he will someday. In other words, don't be talked down to!

When we were both married, our wives became good friends and we continued to grow closer to each other.

When John died, these words that we had spoken together so often at Sunday school came back to me: "And now, may the Lord watch between me and thee while we are apart, one from the other."

Don continues to remember brother John:

JOHN WAS AN accomplished cellist. His first cello was only half-size. He and I both studied with Paul Kotz; then John went on to study with Elwood Mueller. The 1940 picture of the La Salle-Peru High School Orchestra shows John in first chair of the cello section with Lindy sitting next to him, and I'm holding down first chair of the violin section. By now, John had a full-size cello that eventually was passed on to his daughter, Janet.

L-P Orchestra 1940 TOP: **Don, first-chair violin;** BOTTOM: **John, first-chair cello, with Lindy to his right**

One day when Lindy and I were living in Kirkwood, Missouri, I had a phone call from John. He asked me if I'd be interested to work with him on his Drive Across Gate business. I was working for the American Car and Foundry Company and was about ready to find another job. I drove up to Perry, Iowa, and looked over the situation. John, with the help of our dad, Thurman, had some good jigs and fixtures made that, when properly used, insured a good product.

Production wasn't the problem—sales was the problem. John was a good salesman, but the farmers he was trying to sell his gates to were frugal businessmen. This business failed, and John and Roseann moved back to La Salle.

John convinced Dad to start planting Christmas trees out on the farm. I was still living in Kirkwood when the first planting took place. The state of Ohio furnished the tiny trees free.

Lindy, baby Donalyn, and I drove all night to be on hand for this big event. There were eventually fifty thousand trees planted in the ravines and gullies of the farm. Dad's goal had been to leave the farm in better shape than he had found it when he and Mom moved back from Easton, Pennsylvania. Dad certainly accomplished this goal with the help of brother John.

Doretta's Buick

"WOULD YOU HAVE Fat bring some tools or something when you come to visit?" Doretta asked my wife. "It seems I've run over something that splashed on the car bumpers and I can't seem to wipe it off. He'll know what to bring to take it off. It looks like hard mud or something."

My wife dutifully passed the word on to me, and I gathered up my usual box of polishes, cleaners, spray cans of touch-up paint, rust removers, and electric grinding equipment. Seemed like a routine I had set up for caring for Doretta's car.

Doretta was my mother-in-law, my wife's mother. She was pretty old to be driving; besides she never was very good at it. She loved her little Buick, though, and it kept her

1975 Buick Skylark

independent. She lived alone in the country. The car was in my care. I saw to it that it had winter tires, summer tires, that it ran reasonably well, and that it looked nice. Each year I would clean it up so it would make another season in relatively good shape. The car looked pretty good for its age.

When we arrived at Doretta's, some four hundred plus miles away, I was shocked to see the Buick. It was covered with cement, hard cement, from front to back halfway up the sides. The rear bumper was caked with cement over an inch thick. The underside of the car was coated like rust prevention. Both rear springs were broken, I quickly found out when I drove the car. It was obvious I had a huge job ahead of me, and my tools were not adequate for the task. So I improvised and went to work.

Three days later the car looked pretty good again. Of course, some of the cement was permanent. But Doretta was extremely pleased.

"Just what happened, Mom?" I casually asked.

"Well, I was driving to De Pue one afternoon when I came upon a crew of workers along the highway. As usual, they were all standing around with no one working; they were just standing there looking at the road. There was no flagman or barriers put up, so I just drove on. I almost got stuck! Really, they should have had a detour or something so people wouldn't have to drive in wet cement, don't you think? And when I got to the other end, there was an awful bump!"

"Didn't they even try to stop you?"

"Oh no! They all waved me on, at least that's what it looked like, and they were all waving at me. I waved back."

Well, the story isn't over yet. Would you believe that a year later Doretta asked my wife if I'd bring those tools again next time we visit? Yes, she did it again. I didn't even ask.

My Pal John Wacker
by Don Huling

John Wacker

ONE OF MY first memories of you, John, was in grade school. Your folks had bought you riding britches to wear to school, which I though were pretty cool. I drew a picture of what they looked like and asked my mom if she could sew a pair for me. She did not think much of that idea, so I never got my riding britches.

One thing I did get to do with you a few years later was to attend the first National Boy Scout Jamboree in Washington, D.C. The year was 1937, and the country was slowly emerging from the Great Depression. Our family was lucky that my dad had worked steadily through this period as plant engineer for the Alpha Cement Company. My parents, who were both frugal, had taught us as children to save our money. But when the opportunity came to spend two hundred dollars to go to the Jamboree, my parents let me draw my savings out of your dad's bank and sign up.

We both had been in Scouting for only a few months. The Jamboree had been planned for 1935 when we were not yet Boy Scouts, but it didn't actually occur until 1937. Now we had the chance to go. My Jamboree Certificate of Identification No. 18965 reads as follows: Donald J. Huling of La Salle, Ill. is an accredited member of an official contingent at the National Jamboree in Washington, D.C. June 30–July 9, 1937. Countersigned on behalf of the Local Council by Lloyd Shafer. We were issued ribbons that we wore to identify us and help us get back to our troop location as Region VII, Section G, Troop 31.

Before John and I left home for Washington, we were given clock dials from Westclox in Peru and marbles from the glass company in Ottawa to trade at the Jamboree with other Scouts from all over the U.S.A. We didn't do very well until you and I came up with a great idea. We took a hammer and broke the marbles into pieces that sort of glistened. When we told other kids how we had smuggled these precious stones out of a well-guarded cave, they became quite valuable, and we did OK with our trades.

You and I were members of Troop 2, which was sponsored by the Congregational Church of La Salle. Harry Sweger had been very active in both organizations. Harry's younger brother, John, took over as Scoutmaster when Harry stepped down. John was followed by Ed Cox, who was Scoutmaster while you and I were active in the troop.

We advanced through the ranks of Tenderfoot, Second Class, First Class, Star, Life, and Eagle pretty much in unison. You qualified for Eagle before I did, but I was determined to get the Lifesaving merit badge by the end of the summer of 1940 so we could receive our Eagle awards together.

Part of the Lifesaving test was to jump into the Vermillion River fully clothed and save a "drowning" person. The drowning person was Marion Lepich, who allowed no shortcuts. I threw my shoes into the rowboat that I had jumped out of, took off my trousers and shirt, and swam over to Marion, who was thrashing in the water. We had been taught never to approach a drowning person face to face, but to come up to him from behind. I dove underwater and felt which way Marion's toes were pointing, then came up out of the water from behind. I towed him to the rowboat and passed the last hurdle to becoming an Eagle. I later found out the rowboat was standing by in case they had to rescue me from drowning.

One of the benefits for getting the highest award in Scouting was a trip to Canada with our Scout Executive, Lloyd Shafer. There were about eight of us who made the trip in a large limo passenger car with four rows of seats. We drove to Chicago where we boarded a ferry that took us to Muskegon, Michigan. It was an all-night trip, and I remember we were so excited that we didn't sleep much during the crossing. We crossed over to the Upper Peninsula at Mackinac and then on into Ontario, Canada, by way of Sault Ste. Marie. We visited a beautiful waterfall about fifty miles into Canada, then turned tail and raced back to the ferry that was just getting ready to leave for Chicago. You and I sat in the backseat of the limo and had fun poking each other while Lloyd poured on the gas. Life was full of adventures, and we were sure having our share of them.

Both of our families were active in the Congregational Church, which had an outstanding choir director. Mrs. Arnold Wilson, whose husband was an executive at Westclox, had studied music back East and formed the original three choirs. The mothers were well-organized and came up with different colored robes for each group. The children's choir wore red and white robes; purple was for the high-school choir, and black for the adults. Those robes are still hanging in the cabinet in the parlor of the Congregational Church. This music program was continued under Hazel Bett.

We were taught the hesitation walk processional that might be called a dance step today. Every Thursday after school was choir practice. Flag bearers led the children's choir to the pews on each side of the church. Their primary job was to signal the kids to be seated and to stand at the correct time. I have a picture of the whole choir taken by Max Freudenburg, which shows you and me holding the flags. We look so angelic.

We really weren't angels—just two boys growing up in middle-class America having fun and adventures. Things were not quite so nice for our generation in Europe. That was too far away for us to be concerned.

We pulled a couple of pranks that got us into trouble, but only ended with a scolding and a promise not to do it again. One involved throwing snowballs at the city bus after a Scout meeting on Monday night. The troop at the Methodist Church told the police who was doing it, and they caught you, Fred Schmoeger, and me in the act. They took us down to the police station and put us in separate rooms where you and I confessed. Fred insisted he was innocent and didn't tell the truth until the next morning after being behind bars all night. He called us "Stoolies," but that didn't keep the three of us from going on to more adventures.

The next was a doozie. You and Bates, as we called Fred, had skipped school and ridden your bikes out to Mitchell's Grove. We all had BB guns in those days, which you and Bates had taken along and used to shoot a farmer's chicken. Somehow you guys were caught stark-naked by the farmer as you were trying to cook the chicken over an open fire. The farmer was plenty mad and grabbed all of your clothes. Then he demanded you pay one dollar for the chicken you had killed and were trying unsuccessfully to cook.

How were you going to get the money when he had all of your clothes? You finally worked out a compromise. He gave you back your underwear so you could go up to his house to make a phone call and not embarrass his wife. That's when I got involved in the adventure. You called me.

I was troop treasurer and had about five dollars that I kept at home for emergencies. This certainly qualified as an emergency. I took a dollar, jumped on my bike, and came to your rescue.

Another prank we pulled was barricading the conference room door in the high-school library. By this time we were both freshmen at LPO Junior College, which shared facilities with the high school. I had learned the trick of letting a certain length rod, like a broomstick, slip behind a door as we carefully exited the room. Miss Cummings confronted us, and we readily confessed. Our punishment was four laps around the track each night before football practice, as we had both tried out for the team under Bo Burris. We never got into a game except as water boys because we were both too small. The running of laps put us in good condition and might have been providential as you will see as I finish this story.

Elizabeth Cummings

Merwyn "Bo" Burris

My brother John, you, and I went hunting for ducks late one day in November. The ducks were starting to circle and land in a cornfield down by the Peru slew. You were first in line, my brother John was next, and I was bringing up the rear as we walked down the row. We had repeating shotguns that reloaded automatically after being shot. We all fired as a couple ducks flew over us, but we missed.

As we continued forward up the row, my brother stubbed his foot on a cornstalk and accidentally fired his gun—right into your right buttock. Cool heads prevailed as we dropped our guns and helped you out of the field. I kept saying only a few buckshots had hit you, but I was scared to death it might be more serious.

Miraculously a game warden met us as we emerged from the field. We were not supposed to be hunting that late in the day. Fortunately he sized up the situation immediately and rushed you to the Peru hospital where the fight to save your life began.

I went on to join the Ninth Army Air Force in Europe. You couldn't because of your injury. I have often though that with your good eyesight, intelligence, and personality, you might have been made a pilot. About one-third of our pilots lost their lives in World War II. I believe it was God's plan to use your life to better mankind rather than lose it as cannon fodder. I thank God things worked out like they did.

The Carysville Campground

MY GREAT-AUNT Jenny (Mary Jane Huling Williams, 1870–1968) was born in a log cabin on a farm near Carysville, Ohio, the seventh of nine children of the ninth generation of Hulings in America. (See picture on page 211.) Her father, my great-grandfather James Huling, did well by clearing the land, selling the timber after running it through his sawmill, and farming.

Aunt Jenny's two brothers were educated to about grade four before being needed to help their dad, but the seven sisters continued their educations into college.

Aunt Jenny married a lawyer and lived in Columbus, Ohio, starting about 1896. She had plans, however, to teach the community around Carysville about God and the Bible and prepared herself to do so in her studies.

When Jenny's mother, also named Mary Jane, died, Jenny asked for and acquired two acres of land at the corner of the home property, where two highways met. This is where she would build her tabernacle and campground.

The campground was completed with small cottages, a dining hall, and a well for water. All the buildings were painted white and had red tarpaper roofs. The campground was surrounded by a white rail fence above which, at the corner of the busy intersection, was a billboard, also white, on which was painted "CAMP MEETING AUG _____" in red. The blank in the sign would be filled in as soon as Aunt Jenny had selected the two weeks she thought best for the local farmers to have completed filling their barns with hay to feed their cattle all winter.

One more thing . . . the bell! Every evening about an hour before the camp meetings took place, a bell about the size of the Liberty Bell would ring out the news for a radius of two or more miles.

As a boy, I spent summers at my grandfather's farm, which had also been part of the home property. The home farm had been divided into four parcels: Aunt Jenny's two acres, Grandfather's 149 acres, Uncle Charlie's 139 acres, and eighty acres sold. At the time the home farm was divided, there was some dissention among the nine heirs, and this lasted for many years but eventually healed. As I was not a part in the disagreements, I became fond of all of my great-aunts and -uncles, and because of that I like to think I may have helped bring them together from time to time during their healing process.

When I was thirteen, I became good pals with Bobby, Aunt Jenny's grandson. Aunt Jenny was raising Bob because his parents had died when he was quite young. Although Bob was four years my junior, he needed a friend, and so did I. I was the only one of my family spending the summer on the farm, the campground was within walking distance, and Aunt Jenny needed help delivering fliers announcing the upcoming event in August, so she and her son Sam would pick me up at the farm and take me to Sidney, Piqua, Urbana, or Quincy to deliver fliers to homes and place them under windshield wipers of cars. Bob and I became good runners doing this.

Back at the campground, Bob and I would be fed in the dining hall with all the folks who appeared at mealtime. There was always enough to eat. Folks from the area would bring food as part of their support. There were people who cooked, people who pushed lawn mowers, people who painted buildings, guest speakers, musicians, hungry people on their journey to find work, and sometimes farmers who wanted to stop by and say hello at lunchtime. All were welcomed.

After lunch Bob and I usually watched the men work, climbed trees, or tried to get Sam's crystal radio to receive sound. One of the people Bob and I got to know quite well was Joseph Kizer. Joseph was Aunt Jenny's sister Maggie's son, so he was a cousin of both of us. He was a nice young man who told us stories as he painted or nailed tarpaper on roofs. We spent a lot of time with him. The next year, he drowned.

The big August day would come! The bell would sing out, and sure enough, people would arrive before the sun went down. The piano in the tabernacle would ring out great lively music that had a definite ragtime touch to it. Folks would greet folks they hadn't seen since the year before. Sam played a trumpet when hymns were sung, and they were sung with great enthusiasm! If folks could sing harmony, they did so, and if they could sing loud, they did so, and if they sang off-key, they did so, and no one minded at all.

Both Sam, who was a minister, and Aunt Jenny preached. I was not too young to realize they were preaching strong sermons whose messages were to straighten up, quit sinning, follow the gospel teachings of Christ and the apostles, and obey the Ten Commandments! They were not what we would today call liberal, and I need to thank them for whatever influence they ever had on my life, as I have remembered the direction they were pointing me, and all others, to go and consider myself a conservative who tries to follow the very same teachings they presented to me. I may not have become the type of Christian they would have liked, but I do recall their attempts to impress me.

When I first attended the camp meetings, there were kerosene lanterns hanging from the unpainted rafters of the tabernacle. These were soon (about 1936) replaced with strings of light bulbs. The floor was straw over dirt. Fresh straw was spread every year, and it gave the tabernacle a nice smell.

Bob and I had the habit of catching toads and releasing them during the evening services. We soon tired of that when someone suggested we get more of them to eat the mosquitoes that came in through the top-hinged windows that swung out and were propped up.

Some nights were hot, so hot we sat with two fans, one for each hand, to keep cool. The fans came from Baker Funeral Home in St. Paris, if my memory is correct. Sometimes Aunt Jenny preached and fanned at the same time.

Sometimes a summer storm would come up suddenly, and the hinged windows would have to be lowered. The person out in the rain pulling out the props that held them up would get soaked. We felt secure inside the tabernacle and always had lanterns ready in case of power failure.

Each season there would be guest ministers to preach and lead the services. They were billed as star attractions. There were also soloists, or duos, of singers who would liven up the music. On a few occasions, Aunt Jenny and Sam took Bob and me to scout out talent. Once it was to Indian Lake, Ohio, where we happened to walk through a dance hall to find the person they were looking for, and a New Orleans jazz band was practicing for their evening gig. Many years later (1988), when I sent Sam a recording of our jazz band performing "Syncopated Spirituals," he wrote me that he thought it was "syncopated noise," but I swear he was enjoying the sound that day when I was a kid.

Another time they took me to a town I think was Circleville, where the tabernacle was so huge it required two pianos, one on each side of the podium, to be heard. There were few sound systems in those days, and, if there was one there, it would have been for the speaker. I believe a song leader played the trombone to lead the singing. . . . Could it have been Billy Sunday? It might have been. But those pianos were playing ragtime! And I knew what ragtime was, because Mom played ragtime. The two pianos filled in all the spaces where tempo or sound might fade by adding syncopated notes and rhythm. I wrote Sam I had remembered that. I don't believe he agreed with me.

A few nights after going on trips with Aunt Jenny and Sam, we got back to the campground so late that I slept on a steel cot in one of the cabins, rather than wake up my grandparents on their farm. Late one such night, returning to the campground, Bob and I were asleep in the backseat of the car when lightning struck a huge tree right in front of us. Sam, blinded by the flash, slammed on the brakes, and we slid. By the time he stopped the car, we were sideways in the branches of the fallen tree. The tree might just as well have fallen on us!

The next day at camp meeting, Aunt Jenny gave a word

of thanks to the good Lord that we had been spared, and all of Carysville plus the surrounding area heard about it.

Because of Bob, I also became good friends one summer with cousins Nancy and Polly Williams, who were near my age. I never saw them after that one summer, but I do remember we kids were all taken to The Spot in Sidney for hamburgers.

All my memories of the campground are fond ones . . . except I wish the nine siblings of aunts and uncles could have gotten along better as they aged.

When World War II came, Aunt Jenny had trouble finding help to cut the grass at the campground, so she wrote to my brother John and me in Illinois to see if we were going to spend the summer on the farm. We were but couldn't get there until after the first week in June, so we assured her that if someone would cut the grass until we got there, we could keep it under control.

Well, when we got there, the grass was over a foot tall for half of the area and about six inches tall over the rest. We managed to push the two dull mowers through the short grass but could make no headway in the tall grass. The longer it took us, the worse it got. The more time we spent on tall grass, the less time we could spend on the short grass. The harder we charged into the long grass, the duller the mowers got and the longer it took to cut the short grass. We were in trouble.

Then one hot day, about noon, the state highway tractors that cut the grass on the shoulders of the roads came to rest under a tree by the campground to eat lunch. Brother John approached one of the tractor drivers with sweat pouring off his body and pointed out to him our dilemma. He asked the man to just look at how hard I was working and how futile the task was.

The man had pity on us and after he ate lunch, he drove in to cut the grass for us. He had made about three rounds with his mower when he hit a large rock protruding from the ground and broke his mower. Now he was in trouble, because he was only supposed to cut along the highway, and it was quite apparent he had cut our grass up to the rock. So he drove off to make it look like he had broken down somewhere else, while John and I went and got Grandfather to hitch up the horses and use the hay mower from the farm to finish the job. Grandfather didn't hit any rocks. He said he knew where each rock was from the days when he had farmed that land.

From here on, my story is vague. . . . I don't remember if John and I quit or were fired by Aunt Jenny, but we were defeated by dull mowers, and Aunt Jenny thought we were overcharging her.

Just the other day I drove past the campground and thought it looked like an awful lot of grass to cut with a push mower. Of course, the buildings are all gone now, which makes it look larger. Now, only trees and the well remain . . . an era gone.

I have only seen Bob Williams once since we were kids, and that was at the campground in the spring of 1950, when he was there to help do something, maybe cut the grass. Bob has informed me of family happenings from time to time and at Christmas we exchange greetings. I often wonder if he remembers the good times we had.

※   ※   ※

ACKNOWLEDGMENTS

THANK YOU TO those who have been so generous in sharing their memories and photos for this book:

Bob Kessel at The Igloo
Bruce and Sue Hallen for access to the Ralph Hallen Collection of area photographs
Mary Small at the La Salle County Museum, Utica
La Salle Public Library
Peru Public Library
Kaskaskia Hotel and Conference Center

Special thanks to Jean Hahne Huling, the little girl who with her parents walked past Paul on the way to Fourteenth Street, and to Lindy Marshall Huling, my constant inspiration since the days described in this book.

PHOTO CREDITS

Choir Members of the La Salle Congregational Church, Easter Sunday, 1938. See picture on page 74.

1ST ROW: Helen Wacker, Marlyn Miller, Phylics Flower, Peggy McGonigal, Paula Schmoeger, unknown, Mary C. Mertz, Nancy Hawthorn, Patsy Borngasser, Nancy Schermerhorn, Ann Seaton, Joan Gebhardt, Lois Franson, Marsha Bett, Nancy Gay, Marion Smith and Lindy Marshall.

2ND ROW: Jim Hawthorne, Bradley Chase, Harry Nelson, Tommy Seaton, unknown, Billy McClary, Jack Whittle, Bobby Esmond, Strawn Gay, Tyler Goodman, Ralph Thompson, Paul Huling, Max Freudenberg, Kenneth Thompson, Bill Gebhardt, and Edmond Goodman.

3RD ROW: June Wilson, Marcella Freudenberg, Mary Helen Bassett, Lois Floyd, Francis Jane Carrell, Lois Jenkins, Florence Loomis, Betty Mae Brewer, Lois Culver and Mary Wacker.

4TH ROW: John Wacker (Flag Bearer), Marjorie Cate, unknown, Dorothy Wolf, Edna Allen, Janice Currie, Susan Jane Duncan, Jean Billard, Norma Warren, Dorthy Kupack, Mary Jane Duncan, Shirley Bane, Marjorie Burt, Elizabeth Loomis, Portia Harris, Jean Korn, and Donald Huling (Flag Bearer).

LAST ROW: Hazel Bett, Choir Director, Rev. George McClary, and Mildred Taylor, Organist.

Contingent of Draftees–Feb. 23, 1943. See picture on page 154.

FRONT ROW, L TO R: Donald Huling (leader), Robert Tadych, Joseph Niewinski, Frank Wasik, Edward Washkowiak, William Watson, Leo Jesiolowski, and Bernard Buczkowski.

SECOND ROW: Raymond Klimek, John Loebach, Walter Joop, Albert Mecozzi, Dominic Arbise, Roy Kurkowski, Harry Gribbin, Frank Bratkovich, and Floyd Zuchora.

THIRD ROW: Walter Bruski, Theodore Yelich, Robert Waszkowiak, Louis Visnikar, William Skoporc, Louis Martuzzo, Jerome Kowalczyk, Peter Siembab, Albert Marincic, and Joseph Cielaszyk.

FOURTH ROW: Andrew Sorrentino, Dominic Pagoria, Eugene Pioli, William Leland, Joseph Plawny, Edward Kopacz, Frank Bregant, Theodore Zmudka, and Darwin Zevnik.

FIFTH ROW: Joseph Martinjak, Andrew Hart, Robert Bradley, William Baker, Daniel Mertes, William R. Cosgrove, Harry Noel, John Turri, and Robert Hornecker.

TOP ROW: John Roliardi, Stephen Kasap, William Yazbes, Richard Johns, Ross Pagoria, and James Atilano.

Contingent of Draftees–Feb. 23, 1943. See picture on page 155.

FRONT ROW: Ryan Cawley, John Kelly, Paul Morrow, Clarence Volk, John Clausen, Theodore Urbanski, and Gilbert Hobnick.

SECOND ROW: Glen Mauritzen, Richard McBride, Charles Bulfer, Patrick Grimshaw, Louis Delfi, Clarence Sapienza, Kenneth Wardynski, Robert Urban, and Stanley Antanitus.

THIRD ROW: Donald Lennox, Robert Zimmerman, Peter Sampo, Edward Mrowicki, Frank Maggio, Frederick Bosshart, and Irvin Hahn.

FOURTH ROW: Walter Szymovicz, Allen Green, Ken Bleck, Vince Urbino, James Torchia, Samuel Torchia, Leo Zurinski, and George Schuetz.

TOP ROW: George Kobold, Richard Kaszynski, Leonard Staab, Warren Hammerich, Robert Mindock and Chester Hart.

INDEX

Photographs indicated in *bold italic*

Four Corners, 127
Fourteenth Street, 31
Franson, Lois, *74*
Freebairn, Anna Jean, *24*
Freebairn, Donald, *24*
Freebairn, Tom, *24*
Freebairn, Wesley, *24*
Freudenberg, Abby, 14
Freudenberg, Marcella, 205, 206; *74*
Freudenberg, Maximilian, 15
Freudenberg, Maxwell, 14-18, 95,
    107, 194, 197, 205, 206, 241; *15,
    17, 74, 88, 206*
Freudenberg Studio, 14-15, 205
Gay, Nancy, *74*
Gay, Strawn, 72-74; *72, 74*
Gebhardt, Bill "Gabby," 12, 32,
    127, 129-130; *32, 74*
Gebhardt, Joan, 206; *74*
General Motors Corporation, 165
Ginsburg, Nate, 194
Ginsburg, Sadie, 95, 194
Glenn, Loretta, 196
Golden, Jean, 204
Gooding Street, 70, 105, 132, 134,
    199, 200
Goodman, Edmond, *74*
Goodman, Tyler, 145-147; *74, 146*
Goose Pond, 12
Green, Allen, *155*
Green River Ordinance defense
    plant, 170
Gribbin, Harry, *154*
Grimshaw, Patrick, *155*
Gunn Avenue, 119
Hack, Ed, 30
Hahn, Irvin, *155*
Hahne, Bill, *31*
Hahne, Doretta, 237
Hahne, Jean, 31, 34 107, 184-185,
    190, 229; *31, 108*
Hahne, Mr. and Mrs., 30-31
Hall High School, 207

Hammerich, Warren, *155*
Hanley, Joe, 195
Hanley, Leo, 195
Hanley, Margaret, 195
Harker, Jack, *143*
Harl, Mrs., 209
Harl, Eljean, 206
Harl, Sidney, 207
Harris, Dawn, 107
Harris, Portia, 107; *74*
Hart, Andrew, *154*
Hart, Chester, *155*
Hart, Wilbur, 47, 54, 57-58, 61, 63,
    65-66, 68-70, 131, 216, 217; *46*
Haugen, Christie, 229
Haugen, Connie, 229
Haugen, Edward, 229; *229*
Haugen, James, 229
Hawthorn, Nancy, *74*
Hawthorne, Fred, 122
Hawthorne, Jim, *74*
Hawthorne, Grandmother, 68-69,
    96, 97, 121; *67*
Heart, Dale, 230
Hegeler Park, 78, 195
Henderson family, 202
Hess, Frank "Fritz," 123-124; *123*
Hess, Jack, 123
Hicks Park, 124-125
Hill, Ruth, *24*
Hobnick, Gilbert, *155*
Hornecker, Robert, *154*
Horner, "Jug," 138
Huling, Agnes "Mom," 3, 5-7,
    25-26, 34-36, 40-42, 62, 79, 93,
    103, 104, 118, 120-122, 126,
    151-152, 209, 218-221, 226, 227,
    230, 232, 248; *49, 108, 220*
Huling, Alice, 19-20, 64, 119, 121,
    207, 215, 219, 221, 227-230; *11,
    49, 208, 227, 229*
Huling, Charles, 13, 62, 209, 213,
    214, 215, 244; *211, 222*

Huling, Clare, *211*
Huling, Donald, 3, 5-7, 15, 19, 35-36, 62, 64-65, 76, 83, 90, 94-97, 103, 107, 111, 151, 197, 200, 204, 205, 206, 207, 219, 226, 227, 232, 234; *3, 11, 17, 46, 49, 74, 88, 108, 122, 154, 208, 212, 215, 217, 222, 227, 236*
Huling, Don as AUTHOR, 11, 37, 117, 118, 123, 130, 132, 134, 137, 221, 230, 235, 239
Huling, Donalyn, 226-227
Huling, Janet 235
Huling, James Milton, 209-210, 213; *211*
Huling, Jean—SEE Hahne, Jean
Huling, Jean as AUTHOR, 177, 179
Huling, John, 13, 17, 35-36, 37, 56, 62, 65, 77-79, 103, 107, 111, 119, 124, 140, 152-153, 162, 205, 207, 209, 219, 221, 224, 227, 231-232, 236, 243; *49, 108, 208, 217, 222, 235, 236*
Huling, John Henry, 13, 43-44, 47, 55, 57, 61, 63, 118, 131-132, 152-153, 160-162, 209-218, 244, 250; *49, 59, 211, 212, 217*
Huling, Laura, SEE Ashmore
Huling, Margaret "Maggie," SEE Kizer
Huling, Mary Jane (NEE Bowersock), 209, 213, 244; *211*
Huling, Mary Jane SEE Williams
Huling, Mary Virginia, 227
Huling, Nora SEE Baker
Huling, Paul, 13, 37, 55, 108, 119, 138, 165, 219, 221, 227; *5, 17, 49, 74, 75, 88, 108, 146, 164, 181, 208, 217, 222*; SEE ALSO "Fat," "Laundry Fat"
Huling, Orpha, *211*
Huling, Paul (SON), 199
Huling, Roseann, 236

Huling, Sarah Ann "Sally," 224; *211*
Huling, Sarah Virginia "Jenny," 43-44, 47, 58, 60, 62, 63-64, 118, 131-132, 152-153, 160-162, 212, 216 218; *49, 212*
Huling, Silvia, 62
Huling, Thurman "Dad," *ix*, 4, 7, 9-10, 11-14, 19-21, 34, 36, 37-42, 57, 62, 79, 84, 86, 90-91, 99, 114-116, 118-119, 121, 126, 151-152, 157, 196, 197, 209, 211, 213, 218, 219, 221, 230, 232, 234, 236; *49, 55, 108, 115, 164, 212, 217, 220, 222*
Huling, Vickyle, 138, 140; *215*
The Igloo, 109-111, 113, 120-121, 124, 125, 132, 139-140, 142, 170; *141, 144*
Illinois and Michigan Canal, 81-82
Illinois River, 12, 82, 142, 199
Jenkins, Lois, *74*
Jensen, Mr., 226
Jensen's Jewelry Store, 205, 226
Jesiolowski, Leo, *154*
Johns, Richard, *154*
Joliet Street, 95, 104, 144, 194, 196, 197, 200, 204
Johnson, Loraine, *24*
Joop, Walter, *154*
Jorgenson family, 199
Kasap, Stephen, *154*
Kaskaskia Hotel, 27, 30, 140, 193
Kasprowitz, Mike, 114, 116-117
Kaszynski, Richard, *155*
Kelly, John, *155*
Kilmer Street, 200
King, Juliet, 177-179; *178*
Kizer, Joseph, 246
Kizer, Maggie Huling, 222, 246; *211*
Klimek, Raymond, *154*
Kline, Herbie, 200
Kobold, George, *155*

"Sister Jean" the ragtime queen and "Laundry Fat"

This duo with the unlikely names began playing in Illinois, then moved to Brazil, where they were "discovered" as American jazz musicians. Performing as members of "The Saints' Jass Band," they appeared on television, at jazz festivals, for commercials, and at clubs. Returning to the States, they located in Ohio and began spreading the good feeling their music promoted. Their repertoire included pieces from all the major ragtime composers (Scott Joplin, James Scott, Joseph Lamb, and more) as well as their own original songs and an occasional boogie or blues number.